KENNETH BURKE

Kenneth Burke's vast body of theoretical work has important implications for fields as diverse as literary criticism, philosophy, linguistics, politics, anthropology and sociology. Until recently this fascinating work has had a larger reputation than it has had a readership.

Kenneth Burke: Rhetoric and Ideology is a lucid and accessible introduction to the work of a major twentieth-century thinker. By considering Burke as a reader and writer of narratives and systems Bygrave is able to focus on the relationship between language, ideology and action and to mount a claim that Burke not only anticipates current arguments but is a powerfully original thinker in his own right.

This book reinstates Burke into contemporary cultural theory, introducing students of literature and cultural studies to the exciting range of ideas opened up by his work.

CRITICS OF THE TWENTIETH CENTURY

General Editor: Christopher Norris,
University of Wales, College of Cardiff

KENNETH BURKE

Rhetoric and Ideology

Stephen Bygrave

London and New York

First published 1993
by Routledge
11 New Fetter Lane, London EC4P 4EE

Simultaneously published in the USA and Canada
by Routledge
29 West 35th Street, New York, NY 10001

Typeset in 10 on 12 point Palatino by ROM Data Corporation Ltd.,
Falmouth, Cornwall
Printed in Great Britain by T. J. Press (Padstow) Ltd., Padstow,
Cornwall

British Library Cataloguing in Publication Data

A catalogue record for this
book is available from the
British Library

Library of Congress Cataloging in Publication Data
Bygrave, Stephen –
Kenneth Burke: rhetoric and ideology / Stephen Bygrave.
p. cm. — (Critics of the twentieth century)
Includes bibliographical references and index.
1. Burke, Kenneth, 1897– .2. Philosophy, Modern—United
States—20th century. 3. Rhetoric—Philosophy.
4.Literature—Philosophy. I. Title. II. Series: Critics of the
twentieth century (London, England)
B945.B774B94 1993
191—dc20
92-28019

ISBN 0-415-02211-8

Contents

Editor's foreword

The twentieth century has produced a remarkable number of gifted and innovative literary critics. Indeed it could be argued that some of the finest literary minds of the age have turned to criticism as the medium best adapted to their complex and speculative range of interests. This has sometimes given rise to regret among those who insist on a clear demarcation between 'creative' (primary) writing on the one hand, and 'critical' (secondary) texts on the other. Yet this distinction is far from self-evident. It is coming under strain at the moment as novelists and poets grow increasingly aware of the conventions that govern their writing and the challenge of consciously exploiting and subverting those conventions. And the critics for their part – some of them at least – are beginning to question their traditional role as humble servants of the literary text with no further claim upon the reader's interest or attention. Quite simply, there are texts of literary criticism and theory that, for various reasons – stylistic complexity, historical influence, range of intellectual command – cannot be counted a mere appendage to those other 'primary' texts.

Of course, there is a logical puzzle here, since (it will be argued) 'literary criticism' would never have come into being, and could hardly exist as such, were it not for the body of creative writings that provide its *raison d'être*. But this is not quite the kind of knock-down argument that it might appear at first glance. For one thing, it conflates some very different orders of priority, assuming that literature always comes first (in the sense that Greek tragedy had to exist before Aristotle could formulate its rules), so that literary texts are for that very reason possessed of superior value. And this argument would seem to find commonsense support in the difficulty of thinking what 'literary criticism' could *be* if it seriously renounced all sense of the distinction between literary and critical texts. Would it not then find itself in the unfortunate position of a discipline that had willed its own demise by declaring its subject non-existent?

But these objections would only hit their mark if there were indeed a special kind of writing called 'literature' whose difference from other kinds of writing was enough to put criticism firmly in its place. Otherwise there is nothing in the least self-defeating or paradoxical about a discourse, nominally that of literary criticism, that accrues such interest on its own account as to force some fairly drastic rethinking of its proper powers and limits. The act of crossing over from commentary to literature – or of simply denying the difference between them – becomes quite explicit in the writing of a critic like Geoffrey Hartman. But the signs are already there in such classics as William Empson's *Seven Types of Ambiguity* (1928), a text whose transformative influence on our habits of reading must surely be ranked with the great creative moments of literary modernism. Only on the most dogmatic view of the difference between 'literature' and 'criticism' could a work like *Seven Types* be counted generically an inferior, sub-literary species of production. And the same can be said for many of the critics – Kenneth Burke among them – whose writings and influence this series sets out to explore.

Some, like Empson, are conspicuous individuals who belong to no particular school or larger movement. Others, like the Russian Formalists, were part of a communal enterprise and are therefore best understood as representative figures in a complex and evolving dialogue. Then again there are cases of collective identity (like the so-called 'Yale deconstructors') where a mythical group image is invented for largely polemical purposes. (The volumes in this series on Hartman and Bloom should help to dispel the idea that 'Yale deconstruction' is anything more than a handy device for collapsing differences and avoiding serious debate.) So there is no question of a series format or house-style that would seek to reduce these differences to a blandly homogeneous treatment. One consequence of recent critical theory is the realization that literary texts have no self-sufficient or autonomous meaning, no existence apart from their after-life of changing interpretations and values. And the same applies to those *critical* texts whose meaning and significance are subject to constant shifts and realignments of interest. This is not to say that trends in criticism are just a matter of intellectual fashion or the merry-go-round of rising and falling reputations. But it is important to grasp how complex are the forces – the conjunctions of historical and cultural motive – that affect the first reception and the subsequent fortunes of a critical text. This point has been raised into a systematic programme by critics like Hans-Robert Jauss, practitioners of so-called 'reception theory' as a form of historical hermeneutics. The volumes in this series will therefore be concerned not only to expound what is of lasting significance but also to set these critics in the context of present-day argument and debate. In some cases (as with Walter Benjamin) this debate takes the form of a struggle for interpretative power among exponents or disciplines with sharply opposed ideological interests. Such controversies cannot simply be ignored for the sake of achieving a clear and balanced account. They point to unresolved tensions and problems which are there in the critic's work as well as in the rival appropriative readings. In the end there is no way of drawing a neat methodological line between 'intrinsic' questions (what the critic really thought) and those other, supposedly 'extrinsic' concerns that have to do with influence and reception history.

The volumes will vary accordingly in their focus and range of coverage. They will also reflect the ways in which a speculative approach to questions of literary theory has proved to have striking consequences for the human sciences at large. This breaking-down of disciplinary bounds is among the most significant developments in recent critical thinking. As philosophers and historians, among others, come to recognize the rhetorical complexity of the texts they deal with, so literary theory takes on a new dimension of interest and relevance. It is scarcely appropriate to think of a writer like Derrida as practising 'literary criticism' in any conventional sense of the term. For one thing, he is as much concerned with 'philosophical' as with 'literary' texts, and has indeed actively sought to subvert (or deconstruct) such tidy distinctions. A principal object in planning this series was to take full stock of these shifts in the wider intellectual terrain (including the frequent boundary disputes) brought about by critical theory. And, of course, such changes are by no means confined to literary studies, philosophy and the so-called 'sciences of man'. It is equally the case in (say) nuclear physics and molecular biology that advances in the one field have decisive implications for the other, so that specialized research often tends (paradoxically) to break down existing divisions of intellectual labour. Such work is typically many years ahead of the academic disciplines and teaching institutions that have obvious reasons of their own for adopting a business-as-usual attitude. One important aspect of modern critical theory is the challenge it presents to these traditional ideas. And lest it be thought that this is merely a one-sided takeover bid by literary critics, the series will include a number of volumes by authors in those other disciplines, including, for instance, a study of Roland Barthes by a philosopher schooled in the American analytic tradition.

We shall not, however, cleave to theory as a matter of polemical or principled stance. The series will extend to figures like F. R. Leavis, whose widespread influence went along with an express aversion to literary theory; scholars like Erich Auerbach in the mainstream European tradition; and others who resist assimilation to any clear-cut line of descent. There will also be authoritative volumes on critics such as Northrop Frye and Lionel Trilling, figures who, for various reasons, occupy an ambivalent or contested place in current critical debate. This study of Kenneth Burke is one fine example of the benefits to be had by exploring the relation between several (conventionally insulated) disciplines of thought. Above all the series will strive to resist that current polarization of attitudes that sees no common ground of interest between 'literary criticism' and 'critical theory'.

CHRISTOPHER NORRIS

Acknowledgements

It is a pleasure to record an inability. Apart from what is owed to those I know only through their writing I cannot separate the personal from the intellectual debts incurred in writing this book. So these acknowledgements are also a dedication: this book is for all the people named here.

Norman and Eileen Bygrave will understand how debt is not just a metaphor: thank you, still. Paul Kenny, Barbara Kastelein, Tony Parr, Paul Titchmarsh and Eugenia Sifakis talked much of this book through with me, even if they didn't realize that was what they were doing. Paul Kenny read most of it as it was written, and Mark Currie the conclusion. Richard Allen, Carolyn Brown, Val Smith and Judith Vincent kept me going at a crucial stage. Frances Gandy taught me a lot about motivation and but for her this book would have been written much sooner, much worse. He will be embarrassed to see it in print but the intellectual energy and fearlessness of Peter Rawlings have been a durable example to me. Michael White put me on wheels, but someone else put me on my feet and most of those named here will know that my biggest debt is owed to someone who works currently for a bank: to Deborah Vitai, and I hope I can keep up with the repayments.

Abbreviations

ATH	*Attitudes Toward History* (1984), 3rd edn (Berkeley and Los Angeles: University of California Press). First published in 1937.
C	*The Selected Correspondence of Kenneth Burke and Malcolm Cowley, 1915-1981* (1990) ed. Paul Jay (Berkeley & Los Angeles: University of California Press). First published 1988.
C-G	'Counter-gridlock: an interview with Kenneth Burke' (1983), *All Area* no. 2 (1983), 6–33.
CR	'Critical response I: methodological repression and/or strategies of containment' (1978), *Critical Inquiry* vol. 5, no. 2 (Winter 1978), 401–16.
CS	Counter-Statement (1968), 3rd edn (Berkeley and Los Angeles: University of California Press). First published 1931.
D	'Dramatism' (1968), in *International Encyclopaedia of the Social Sciences*, ed. David L. Sills (New York: Macmillan and Free Press, 1968), vol. 7, 445–52.
DD	*Dramatism and Development* (1972), Heinz Werner Lecture Series 6 (Barne, Mass.: Clark University Press/Barne Publishers).
DL	'Dramatism and logology' (1985), *Communication Quarterly*, vol. 33, no. 2 (Spring 1985), 89–93.
GM	*A Grammar of Motives* (1969) (Berkeley: University of California Press). First published in 1945.
LAPE	'Linguistic approach to problems of education' (1955), in *Modern Philosophies and Education*, Yearbook of the National Society for the Study of Education LIV, Part 1, ed. Nelson B. Henry (Chicago: University of Chicago Press), 259–303.

LSA	*Language as Symbolic Action: Essays on Life, Literature, and Method* (1966) (Berkeley and Los Angeles: University of California Press).
(N)M/(S)A	'(Nonsymbolic) motion/(symbolic) action' (1978), *Critical Inquiry* vol. 4 (Summer 1978), 809–38.
PC	*Permanence and Change: An Anatomy of Purpose* (1984), 3rd edn, revised (Berkeley: University of California Press). First published in 1935.
PLF	*The Philosophy of Literary Form: Studies in Symbolic Action* (1973), 3rd edn (Berkeley and Los Angeles: University of California Press). First published in 1941.
RM	*A Rhetoric of Motives* (1969) (Berkeley: University of California Press). First published in 1950.
RR	*The Rhetoric of Religion: Studies in Logology* (1970) (Berkeley: University of California Press). First published in 1961.
TwPr	'Twelve propositions by Kenneth Burke on the relation between economy and psychology' (1938), *Science & Society*, II (Spring 1938), 242–9.
WS	'Why satire, with a plan for writing one' (1974), *Michigan Quarterly Review* 13 (Winter 1974), 303–37.

Introduction

Kenneth Burke has nearly twenty pages of 'Postscripts on the negative' in his book *Language as Symbolic Action* (1966) and I need to begin with a negative prescript. This book cannot provide an introduction to the voluminous writings of Kenneth Burke, born in 1897 and still alive and publishing. Burke's earliest publication was in 1916 and it seems likely that the manuscript of *A Symbolic of Motives*, the third volume of a trilogy so far comprising *A Grammar of Motives* (1945) and *A Rhetoric of Motives* (1950), which was substantially finished in the fifties, will be published posthumously. It is not though the scale of the enterprise which makes me demur at introducing Burke within these limits. Burke's own encyclopaedia article on 'Dramatism' remains as good an introduction to his thinking as any, and there are books and articles which do attempt to introduce Burke by abstracting his 'thinking' or 'system' from his writings. The best of them aim to apply what is thus abstracted to reading literary texts (Rueckert 1982; Henderson 1988) or to sociological method (Gusfield 1989a). This book is not such an introduction. Although the first chapter attempts a sort of conspectus of Burke's writings, they are not treated as 'theory' to be applied within the 'practice' of existing disciplines: 'to explain our position', Burke writes in the introduction to *A Grammar of Motives*, 'we shall show how it can be applied' (*GM* xv), and I have mostly been content to read what Burke shows us, hoping that this reading itself will show how pervasive is his example as an interpreter – for it is as an interpreter that I discuss Burke, and as an interpreter in as wide a sense, I hope, as is suggested by his title for the first chapter of *Permanence and Change* (1935): 'All living

1

things are critics.' I argue below that this wide rather than specialized kind of interpretation is fundamental to Burke's sense of 'rhetoric'. So, what I do attempt in this book, and the perspective from which Burke is read, is indicated by its subtitle, 'Rhetoric and ideology'. These are fraught terms, terms to which we shall need to make a continual return. Rhetoric is a term made even more fraught by Burke's redefinitions and extensions of it and ideology is a term on whose usage the only consensus seems to be among those who would reject its use.

Most uses of the term contain centrally the sense that ideology is motivated, in however concealed, contradictory or even unconscious a fashion, by a programme of action. It contains implicitly petitions, imperatives, exhortations and other devices which may serve either to legitimate the interests of a dominant group or to challenge those interests in the name of others. An ideology in fact depends on the devices codified as the set of tropes of a rhetoric. This does not mean that rhetoric and ideology are conterminous but it does mean that where ideology becomes apparent in language it can only ever be understood (as opposed to 'experienced') through interpretation and that the kind of interpretation best suited to it is that which can show the relation of language to action – that is, rhetoric. Of course it is clear that a great deal of rhetorical utterance is not also ideological utterance. Someone who shouts 'Fire!' in a crowded theatre is engaging in the former but not the latter, to cite an example from Terry Eagleton's recent book (Eagleton 1991: 205). Ideology can function unconsciously, and this is true even (or perhaps especially) of a dominant ideology. Where it is recognized however it is recognized through rhetoric. That is to say that it depends on conscious acts of interpretation, and rhetoric can provide the formal strategies of those acts. This need not depend on the truism that *all* language is to some degree rhetorical because the qualification 'to some degree' is insidious: questioning that is the beginning of any inquiry into rhetoric rather than its end. To insist on the self-enclosed rhetoricity of language is a means of evading the ideological questions of the ends it may serve. Eagleton's book has a more pragmatic aim, 'to view ideology less as a particular *set* of discourses, than as a particular set of effects *within* discourses' (Eagleton 1991: 194), which reinserts its workings within the purview of rhetorical study. Much of his book is a history of error – a history of variously deluded attempts to define the workings of ideology, including some about which Eagleton was more enthusiastic in the past, and, latterly, of attempts to deny its usefulness altogether. Some thinkers are more or less exempted from the charge of error: the later Marx, Gramsci, Habermas and, perhaps surprisingly, Freud. Though the term ideology is more or less absent from Freud's writings, psychoanalysis is seen as potentially a powerful discourse of ideological critique:

> Projection, displacement, sublimation, condensation, repression, idealization, substitution, rationalization, disavowal: all of these are at work in the text of ideology, as much as in dream and fantasy; and this is one of the richest legacies Freud has bequeathed to the critique of ideological consciousness.
>
> (Eagleton 1991: 185)

The list of Freudian vocabulary is a list also of a rhetorical vocabulary, the instruments of a critique. Perspective by incongruity, socialization, identification, hierarchy, courtship, transcendence, bureaucratization, act, scene, agent, agency and purpose, logomachy: these are Burke's terms which, I shall argue, are similarly useful instruments of ideological critique.

Thus in seeing Kenneth Burke as an interpreter and as a theorist of interpretation I see him contributing to the possibility of ideological critique rather than to, say, the history of literary criticism. Literary criticism is a discourse which stresses the intrinsic value of the 'content' it claims as its province; Burke has extended study of the 'forms' it treats of into domains of 'content' characteristically alien and even inimical to that discourse. By inhabiting it in order to demonstrate its ideological exclusions and to move beyond them Burke practises what I have called 'critique'. He does so by employing a discourse that is much older and much less confined to the content it produces for itself: I mean rhetoric.

> In part, we would but rediscover rhetorical elements that had become obscured when rhetoric as a term fell into disuse, and other specialized disciplines such as esthetics,

anthropology, psychoanalysis, and sociology came to the fore (so that esthetics sought to outlaw rhetoric, while the other sciences we have mentioned took over, each in its own terms, the rich rhetorical elements that esthetics would ban).

(*RM* xiii)

Traditionally, rhetoric is the activity of persuasion. It is also the *study* of that activity, and we shall need to return to that double sense, but it should be noted here that rhetoric is necessarily transitive. Even where a rhetoric is a static repertory of tropes, these are tropes which aim to persuade someone to do something: persuasion itself might be defined as 'inducement to action'. As with the 'programme of action' incipient in ideology, 'action' may have to be pretty loosely defined. An audience may be 'moved' by some utterance without being moved, as is Mark Antony's audience in *Julius Caesar*, to stage a counter-coup: actions may be deferred, or may only retrospectively come to be seen as the effects of which a given utterance was the cause. Burke's own problematic solution is to split off a purely denotative realm of language-use which he calls 'scientist'. One problem with this is that he finds it necessary to split off this realm for his own analytic purposes while castigating 'scientists' for being deluded enough to think that *they* can do so. Then there is 'action', actual or incipient, produced by rhetorical uses of language, together with 'symbolic action', which is action 'for and in itself' as demonstrated for example in poems and novels. Drama is a different case, furnishing Burke with the literal terms by which, he claims, all action can be described.

It is the status of art which, in an early essay with that title, causes problems for any simple definitions of ideology. Burke rejects the crudity of a base-and-superstructure model just as, we shall see, he rejects the crudity of a cause-and-effect model and will reject too the assumption that what is logically prior is also temporally prior:

In one sense art or ideas do 'reflect' a situation since they are a way of dealing with a situation. When a man solves a problem, however, we should hardly say that his solution is 'caused' by the problem to be solved. The problem may limit somewhat the *nature* of his solution, but the problem can remain unsolved forever unless he *adds* the solution.

(*CS* 80)

Works of art here are seen, in Kantian terms, as being purposive without purpose, as being relatively autonomous. Burke needs his notion that the work of art is supplementary – 'the thing added, – the little white houses in a valley that was once a wilderness' (*CS* x) – in order to resist a claim that works of art are ideological phenomena simply to be 'read off' against economic determinants:

The theory of economic causation seemed to rest upon the assumption that there is only one possible aesthetic response to a given situation, and that this situation is solely an economic one.... Drive the logic of causation to the point where economic determinism becomes cosmic determinism, and the detractors of art are necessarily silenced, for their own detractions become but the output of the universal mill, their preferences mere personal choices devoid of 'absolute' sanction.

(*CS* 80–1)

The slippage from 'causation' to 'determinism' here indicates why Burke is suspicious of notions that art can only be a reflection of economic relations. The relation between 'art or ideas' and the broad 'situation' is an active one. Here, the activity is only an activity of addition; Burke rejects a conception of art as the ideological 'reflection' of the base as too narrow without as yet having worked out a wider definition. The functions of ideology are crucial to Burke's project even where he does not use the word or where he uses it in the more restricted sense he describes here.

Near the beginning of a section on 'Traditional principles of rhetoric' in his *Rhetoric of Motives* Burke appears to reserve the uses of 'persuasion' for instances where there is 'freedom' to be persuaded or not to be persuaded, but finds at once that what he is reserving this from is a wholly determined realm where the only freedom is of the market:

often we could with more accuracy speak of persuasion to 'attitude' rather than persuasion to out-and-out action. Persuasion involves choice, will; it is directed to a man only insofar as he is *free*.... Insofar as [men] *must* do something, rhetoric is unnecessary, its work being done by the nature of things, though often these necessities are not of a natural origin, but come from necessities imposed by man-made conditions ... from the nature of the 'free market'.

(RM 50)

Here the 'nature of things' may be 'man-made', an instance of what the later Marx calls 'reification' or the Roland Barthes of *Mythologies* the overturning of culture into nature: that is, ideology. That is, to use terms I have already employed, Burke will 'inhabit' the terminology of a specialized discourse in order to demonstrate shortcomings it will possess simply because it *is* specialized; and this is what I have called 'critique'. By going on to substitute 'identification' for 'persuasion' as the principle of rhetoric, Burke himself identifies the two realms he at first distinguishes in this quotation. Identification can be exemplified by the strategic alliances between groups whose interests are opposed in order to gain particular ends, but it can also be exemplified locally by a speaker or writer's claims to be like his or her audience in some respect, in order that they might come to 'identify' furthering their interests with furthering his or hers. In the thirties Burke can restate the then-orthodox Marxist model of ideology as a phenomenon of the superstructure. Later, reacting against the determinism that limits such a model, he tends to employ the concept while witholding the name, as here. It seems that volition is a criterion of rhetoric, and determinism a criterion of ideology, yet ideology too is man-made and thus, at least in some 'original' state, produced by 'free' agents. Rhetoric is split from ideology in order to rejoin it. There is then a distinction between rhetorical utterance and its interpretation, though both are called 'rhetoric': otherwise put, rhetoric is a kind of metalanguage as well as a kind of language.

The word rhetoric is used both to mean the activity of employing words for the purposes of persuasion, and to mean the study of that activity (by, for example, making an inventory of the tropes by which persuasion can occur). My own discussion

6

above slips between these uses. This is not deliberate but it is, I think, inevitable. Rhetoric is transitive: it joins utterance to action, and the relation between the two is the product of an act of interpretation which is almost always going to be arguable. This basic point is evident from Burke's own distinctive manner of writing. Rhetoric and ideology are not the same thing, but the latter is not to be understood without the former, and his demonstration of this is one way in which Burke is vitally exemplary.

There are other ways in which Burke has been taken as exemplary and my disagreement with some of them will, I hope, animate this book while my disagreement with others must remain implicit. I shall deal with one particular controversy over how he is exemplary (or whether he ought to be) later in this introduction. This should reinforce my reason for why the book as a whole cannot provide an introduction to Burke. To see him as exemplary or as admonitory is to presume him already understood, or at least explained. The choices and emphases necessary in the exposition of a large and complex corpus such as Burke's would make it foolish to assume (and dishonest to claim) that the exposition could be at once comprehensive and judicious, at once full and value-free. It's worth my restating this truism because Burke would disagree with my emphasis. Discussing him within the frame I have sketched means joining a debate in which Burke himself has intervened, to resist what he sees as the imposition of the term 'ideology' in reading his corpus. (It is what he would call a 'god-term' to which he owes no fidelity.) Since there have been complaints that in reading others Burke imposes his extrinsic (and idiosyncratic) categories upon them, he will be aware of an irony in his own complaints. The ambition and the consistency of Burke's career are startling, and of course we are required to engage his consistent concerns and his own vocabulary, but not necessarily *in* his own vocabulary. I take his work to be exemplary in part for its methodological agility, its demonstration of the possibilities offered by changes in perspective and by analogical reasoning. Reading him can be, as he says of reading Freud, 'suggestive almost to the point of bewilderment' (*PLF* 258), but the suggestions need to be sifted from the bewilderment if our reading is to produce and not merely reproduce effects.

Although I shall isolate a recent controversy over whether Burke is an exemplary kind of ideological critic, there is a continuous history of response to him in the United States; but none here. So one motive for this book is simply to answer a lack: in Britain Burke has hardly been read at all. In the two standard bibliographies there is barely an item which was first published in Britain or by a Briton. I take this to be more than a bibliographical lack. The reasons why Burke has been more or less ignored in this country are similar to the reasons why many have taken him as their antagonist in the States – and this book will be introductory to the extent that I need to reproduce the antagonisms and their occasions – but I am interested in why questions about Burke in America result in some energetic antagonism to, and defences of, his work while in a British context it seems enough that similar questions be posed for it to be self-evident that they are not worth answering.

In America there have been various attempts to appropriate Burke: by old and new New Critics ('If you really understand Kenneth Burke, you don't need Derrida as much'); as a 'Western Marxist' left off the genealogy; and by those who seek to show that, given native American pragmatism, you don't need either Marx or Freud.[1] There is of course something ironic in the latter kind of appropriation. Burke is known in Britain, if he is known at all, as a thirties Marxist who proleptically tried to 'mix' Marx and Freud before the job could be done properly in sixties Paris and on the American eastern seaboard in the seventies. Burke has not had anything like a conventional academic career, lacking what is usually its minimum entrance requirement – he does not hold even a BA. He is known then as a wild man, an autodidact who requires us to learn his idiolect and his system before we are vouchsafed anything like a set of portable concepts. The sheer range of Burke's work – that, for example, it draws on writers as diverse as Aquinas, Thorsten Veblen, Shakespeare, Bentham, Spinoza, Coleridge, Augustine, William Empson and Adolf Hitler – seems to encourage reading it as though it were handmade, homespun, not to be taken with the seriousness with which, say, Colin Wilson was taken; or to act as a discouragement from reading it at all. British academe would want to know first of all: well, what is he – Philosopher? Anthropologist? Literary critic? Sociologist?

8

For Burke himself, this very question would be evidence of the division of labour, of a proprietorial specialization of discourse. His disavowal of specialization does not have a simply corrective or reformist aim: it is one of the fundamental grounds of his practice, not only fundamental as a means of avoiding the dangers inherent in specialized vocabularies of whatever kind but also fundamental as the prerequisite for the totalizing description of human action he is ambitious to provide. Despite his disdain for most of its products, this remains a nineteenth-century ambition on Burke's part – an ambition to produce if not a Key to all Mythologies then a Bible of Hell, an antinomian rhetoric the ultimate terms of which will be essentially metaphysical and theological rather than contingently historical and political. At the same time, that rhetoric *requires* rather than merely *allows* that the motives for action be seen as relative to the interests of particular groups at particular stages in their history. This requirement results in a continual dialectic of the essential and the contingent; or, to put it another way, a dialectic of ideological demands and the critique of ideology. The need to understand contingent pressures continually threatens to render arbitrary and relative the attempts at systematization, so that Burke considers collecting his essays of the thirties under the Heraclitean rubric 'While everything flows' (*PLF* xvii).

Burke's awareness of, and his employment of, this dialectic is a reason why I take him to be exemplary. If Burke has not been read in Britain, some regard his as an example that has not been followed in America either. At the beginning of an essay on Burke, Fredric Jameson poses the question of why Burke's project should have been so 'utterly without influence' –

the question as to why this immense critical corpus, to which lip service is customarily extended in passing, has – read by virtually everybody – been utterly without influence in its fundamental lessons, has had no following, save perhaps among the social scientists, and is customarily saluted as a monument of personal inventiveness and ingenuity ... rather than as an interpretative model to be studied and a method to be emulated.

(Jameson 1988: 138)

I want to leave this question unanswered, or as a rhetorical question (one to which we already know the answer), while considering a recent debate over whether and how Burke is to be taken as exemplary, to which both Jameson and Burke himself contribute. I am not trying to restage this debate, and certainly not to adjudicate it, but since the terms of the debate influence the frame in which I discuss Burke it will be helpful to tell its story here.

The story begins in September 1977 with an English Institute panel on 'The achievement of Kenneth Burke', chaired by Hayden White and consisting of papers from Angus Fletcher, John Freccero and Fredric Jameson. Jameson's essay was published the following year, in the Spring 1978 issue of *Critical Inquiry*. Jameson's Burke is a 'Freudo-Marxist' who exemplifies an imperative for ideological analysis of all narrative, in part by his failure to carry through such analysis himself. Burke's 'lesson' is the demonstration that narrative is action; his limitation – what Jameson calls his 'strategy of containment' – is an implicit faith in a kind of enlightened reason which retains categories – chiefly that of the autonomous subject – in their place, or *re*places them.

Jameson taxes Burke with 'a strange reluctance to pronounce the word "ideology" itself' (Jameson 1978a: 521) and Burke replies, in the Winter 1978 issue of *Critical Inquiry*, first by documenting his consistent usage of the term, then by taxing Jameson in return with an 'overinvestment' in it. Jameson had concluded by regretting that 'Burke did not want to teach us history, even though he wanted to teach us how to grapple with it' (Jameson 1978a: 523); Burke replies by referring to his book of forty years previously, *Attitudes Toward History*:

> being built around the somewhat indeterminately polar attitudes of acceptance and rejection, my book is stronger on attitude than on history.... As I see the situation, we can have but *attitudes* toward whatever of history is either past or not yet here.
>
> (CR 410)

For Jameson, history is what he elsewhere calls the ' "untranscendable horizon" ' of all acts of interpretation (1981: 10).

He sees Burke's own writings as determined, in their redemptive liberalism, by the Depression, the New Deal and McCarthyism. In reply, Burke attempts to shift the argument from history to the timeless essences of his 'Logology':

> To start not, as per the *Communist Manifesto*, with the class struggle, but with the 'prime' logological (and Socratic?) question, 'What is it to be the typically symbol-using animal?', could only be viewed as 'ideology' in Jameson's thumbs-down sense, even though such a position could go along with much that Marx says about the class struggle. But the flat opposition between 'ideas' as derivative in the Marxist genealogy and formative in Hegel's invites a kind of 'genetic fallacy' whereby overstress upon the *origins* of some manifestation can deflect attention from what it *is*, regardless of what it came from.
>
> (CR 415)

The last point shrewdly reinstates a synchronic dimension as more than just a preliminary to interpretation; but there is as much of exasperation as there is of pragmatism here, and it bespeaks antithetical motives. Burke wants to show that he is not deficient in terms of those things in which Jameson finds him lacking, and at the same time he wants to show that the charge arises from illegitimately imposing terms which are themselves deficient. Jameson's counter-response is printed immediately after Burke's essay. The 'ideology' that Burke documents from his own writings is for Jameson 'most often ... our old friend "false consciousness", so unavoidable a part of the baggage of thirties Marxism' (1978b: 418). It is insufficient not least because, Jameson argues (employing a Burkean trope), 'false' presupposes 'true'; and he reiterates an argument for the functional necessity of a concept of ideology coupled with an argument for the near impossibility of defining it. Burke's concept of symbolic action has been crucial but it under-rates the functions of symbolic action in serving the interests of some group. Thus Jameson inverts Burke's priorities:

> for Burke, the concept of ideology is essentially an instrumental one whose usefulness lies in its effectiveness in

dramatizing the key concept of symbolic action ... [while] I have found the concept of symbolic action a most effective way of demonstrating the ideological function of culture.

(1978b: 421)

In 1981 Jameson's *The Political Unconscious* incorporates a paragraph of his (first) essay on Burke in its lengthy first chapter, 'On interpretation: literature as a socially symbolic act'. The next year, 1982, Jameson's first essay is reprinted in *Representing Kenneth Burke*, edited by Hayden White and Margaret Brose, which contains versions of all three papers given at the English Institute panel five years previously and adds four others including Frank Lentricchia's 'Reading history with Kenneth Burke'. Like Jameson's Burke, Lentricchia's is the writer of the works up to and including *A Rhetoric of Motives* (1950). Like Jameson, he sees in them an 'antidote' to the idealizing tendencies of much literary theory since the thirties, and again like Jameson he sees the significance of Burke's project lying in its provision of a hermeneutic of actions rather than of objects. For Lentricchia though, Burke's 'system' is more positively exemplary in that it can incorporate the historical disruptions of system, which may indeed be its true object. His essay also acknowledges that to justify the claims he makes for Burke would be 'the task of a book-length project', a project fulfilled the following year with the publication of his *Criticism and Social Change*.

Lentricchia's book is partly a kind of supplement to his *After the New Criticism* (1980), which closes by offering accounts of four 'exemplary' careers. These accounts were largely admonitory, the examples were negative; *Criticism and Social Change* offers Burke's career as their positive counterpart. Lentricchia presents Burke as an example of Gramscian optimism for the American humanist prone to the mandarin quietism that results equally from the deconstruction of Paul de Man or from the neopragmatism of Richard Rorty. Political action is not simply a possibility for the literary intellectual but something with which s/he is involved willy-nilly because 'not all social power is literary power, but all literary power is social power' (Lentricchia 1983: 19). This aphorism is in danger of letting the

12

cat in at the back door having thrown it out at the front: if all teaching is necessarily political that may not induce teachers to change what they do, though it may induce them to change the way they regard what they do. A version of ideology which, rather than relating consciousness to material existence, simply collapses the one into the other, may not be sophisticated so much as incoherent. Lentricchia wants to enlist Burke in furthering an optimism of the spirit as well as of the will:

> The lacerating self-contempt of the intellectual, who has been sold an ironic bill of goods called 'powerlessness', is not only premature and excessive: it is unnecessary. For there remains in the act an irreducible contemporaneity, which is its temporal ground and the guarantee of its activity, the sanction of its ability to make something happen.
>
> (Lentricchia 1983: 140)

Lentricchia uses Burke's terms ('act' and 'ground') to affirm the historicity of the present; seen as such, history becomes not a determining dead weight but the prospect and promise of significant action. Lentricchia pleads the case for Burke as a 'Western Marxist' who was not only left out of the line described in Perry Anderson's *Considerations on Western Marxism* (1976), but who can also answer its critique of the divorce of action from theory.

The Kenneth Burke I encounter in this book is related to the ones described by Jameson and by Lentricchia, so the story can draw to a close with each nodding at the other. The paperback edition of *Criticism and Social Change* was issued in 1985 with a postscript by Burke. In 1988 Jameson's essays of 1971–86 are collected in two volumes under the title *The Ideologies of Theory*. His essay on Burke is reprinted with the addition of a footnote reference to *Criticism and Social Change*, archly observing that Lentricchia's Burke 'is a precursor and heroic ancestor whom one would be only too grateful to acknowledge' but reiterating the belief that the political ambiguities of Burke's writings are final, not merely strategic (1988: 197). In 1989 is published *The Legacy of Kenneth Burke*, mostly papers from a conference held at the University of Wisconsin, which contains a transcript of

Burke's speech to the American Writers Congress in 1935, the contemporary record of reactions to it, and 'Analysis of Burke's speech by Frank Lentricchia'. This last is an extract from his book of 1983, which Lentricchia introduces as being 'pretty much the heart' of that book – Burke's rejection by orthodox Communism serving as emblem of his ideological mobility which can however still be called Marxist. As Lentricchia also says, 'I did not write the book in order to answer Fredric Jameson's critique of Burke, but I suppose that's one way of reading what I've done' (Lentricchia 1989: 281).

Like Lentricchia, I am largely concerned in this book with what Burke in a characteristic pun calls his 'thirty-minded' writings. Unlike Lentricchia, I do not argue that Burke is what used to be called a Euro-Marxist, like his contemporary Gramsci, nor that his undoubted prescience in anticipating many of the concerns of radical critics nearer the other end of the century should make him either their hero or their consolation. Thus far I am with Jameson, yet I part company with him elsewhere – where, for example, he charges Burke's 'system' with having 'no place for an unconscious':

> The dramatistic modes ... are all categories of conscious-ness, open to the light of day in classical, well-nigh Aristotelian fashion; the Burkean symbolic act is thus always serenely transparent to itself, in lucid blindness to the dark underside of language, to the ruses of history or of desire.
>
> (Jameson 1988: 151)

I take Burke's optimism to be Gramsci's 'optimism of the will', the counterpart of a 'pessimism of the intellect', rather than a naïvely exclusive faith in daylight reason. What is more striking about Burke's project (especially once we include the work of the last forty years) is the way it anticipates and can even incorporate the objections that might be made to it. This is why, I have suggested, he may be his own best expositor and why charging him with, say, essentialism is rather like – to adopt a bit of folk-rhetoric – charging the Pope with being Catholic. A page earlier, Jameson has had to concede, in reference to the insufficiency of notions of the 'self', that what is paradoxical about Burke's own critical practice in this respect is that he has anticipated many of the fundamental objections to such a rhetoric of self and identity at the same time that he may be counted among its founding fathers.

(1988: 150)

Despite the pervasiveness of this single issue, Jameson does not find this paradox pervading Burke's writings: Burke may, Janus-like, look in two directions at once, and this might be described in many ways, but it cannot be described as 'blindness'.

The first chapter of this book considers Burke as a reader and writer of narratives, as a builder of systems and as their critic. Here the procedure is eclectic: it is to collect some exhibits of Burke's interpretative methods – methods which at their most powerful, I argue, are those of an ideological critic. These exhibits come mainly from the most systematic of Burke's published writings, *A Grammar of Motives* (1945), although the chapter closes by considering a complete essay from a few years earlier. I try to show that Burke's kind of interpretation is not itself eclectic, but is a rhetoric always directed at the 'uses' of discourse. To consider 'use' is to consider context and effect together. Burke's is a methodology of interpretation then which privileges neither the author (as in Romantic aesthetics) nor the audience (as in neoclassical aesthetics). I shall argue that it also refuses, or suspends, the privilege other kinds of theoretical discourse afford themselves by assuming their own distance or immunity from the critique they furnish of their object-discourse. This reflexiveness might of course conclude in paradox, with assertions of undecidability, or in mere play, but these are not Burke's conclusions. Throughout his work he interrogates the procedures by which discourse seeks to legitimate or authorize itself, and I examine a seemingly empirical example from the *Grammar of Motives* in the fourth chapter: what this examination shows, I think, is that though 'grounds', as Burke calls them, continually give way, their residue is the continued rhetorical effort to establish or to re-establish stable 'grounds' rather than being mere play. At the same time, throughout his work also, play is not dismissively 'mere' because in it *drama* figures as a methodology rather than as a source of analogies and examples. So I argue in the second chapter that such a methodology is interactive and dialectic rather than being reflexive and, ultimately, narcissistic. Lentricchia's book is important for, amongst other things, showing that this kind of argument (for the deconstructive wrong turn) need not necessarily be used to reactionary ends. The Burke represented by Lentricchia did not exist, so it was necessary to invent him; but he does more than repair an omission. As he suggests, Burke's project entails a thoroughgoing critique of ideology, a consideration of the claims of narrative itself from the inside. Though I shan't generally point out the way Burke anticipates much of the agenda of subsequent theory, his rhetoric thus addresses itself to what Jürgen Habermas calls the 'legitimation crisis' that afflicts us as we are led to recognize the untenability of the narratives by which we have lived since the Enlightenment. (Burke himself would locate the start of the rot later, in nineteenth-century historicism.)

In presenting Burke from the perspective of work done on him by Fredric Jameson and Frank Lentricchia, I cast him in a role which he would himself refuse, as a historical critic who exemplifies a road not taken for ideological critique. He would refuse such terms, I think, because of arguments he conducted within and then against the Marxism of the thirties; to see our actions and our capacities for understanding as determined by historical forces is for Burke akin to seeing them merely as reflexes, in the way they are seen by behaviourist psychology. As I have already suggested, Burke's own flexible and opportunistic use of history modifies his refusal of such a crude model, just as it must modify the model itself. Burke's argument with determinism, some instances of which I trace in the third chapter, is again dialectical, concerned with the essential and the contingent, the variant and the invariant. We write history, he insists, as well as being written into it; we speak as well as being spoken for. 'Perspective by incongruity', a trope of translating the terms of an argument, has the aim of reconciliation; it puts the materials for tragedy under the sign of comedy.

In *Attitudes Toward History* (1937) Burke calls this mode a 'comic frame', implying by the summarizing term a static category rather different from the evidence of his practice, in which comedy is always something which is won from conflict. That

16

is to say, the term implies something resolved rather than the movement of resolution. (Another way of putting this might be that Burke replaces an idealist's organic metaphor – a metaphor of process – with a materialist's description of action, which is for him no metaphor.) In a preface, written in 1952, to the second edition of his *Counter-Statement* (1931), Burke records 'unqualified delight' at discovering 'that the book begins on the word "perhaps" and ends on the word "norm" ' (*CS* xi), but this book does not come to rest, as do those early books by Burke, on the metaphor of a 'norm'. The fourth chapter tries to confront the alternatives of paradox and tautology which often seem to lie on the other side of the interpretative bounds which Burke transgresses. It tries to show what I have claimed in compressed form in this introduction: that Burke depends upon (and illuminates) a concept of ideology even where the term is absent, or may be denied. It tries to show that the 'grounds' of any interpretative act themselves rest on an act. This implies neither circularity nor an infinite regress. Burke anticipates this deconstructive move, and the move beyond it too. However he is not so much a missing link in Anglo-American theory as an untapped resource. The final chapter suggests that his rhetoric offers a means of reading history as well as of reading *into* history: a means of connecting all sorts of 'symbolic action' to ideology and the programme of palpable action which underlies it. Burke offers resources of critique which we need.

1

Equipment for living

When he was 6 or 7 years old Kenneth Burke was kept off school. It was feared that he had become learning-disabled after falling from a second-storey window. One day his mother bought him a dictionary: 'she gave me the "Good Book" ', Burke has said, 'but with no instructions on how to figure out what was inside it.' Curse and blessing are, as he was to show later, intimately related: 'Lots of kids who learn to read the easy way don't get much out of it, but I had to develop a theory of language!'[1] This is what Burke would call a 'representative anecdote' (*GM* 59–61). The anecdote might recall T. S. Eliot's essay on Blake, describing Blake as having to make up a system out of whatever he had to hand, like Robinson Crusoe, because he was deprived of what Dante was privileged with: the amniotic 'tradition' of medieval Catholicism (Eliot 1934). Such reactionary claims of deprivation would of course miss the point. 'To contemplate our subject', says Burke, 'we must have a terministic equipment that lends itself to such contemplation' (*GM* 319). This is like the cry of Blake's Los: 'I must create a System or be enslav'd by another Man's.' (The analogy of Burke's difficulty or idiosyncracy might be pushed further: where Blake was working with the censorship and repression of the printed word imposed by the 'gagging acts' of the 1790s Burke was publishing in the era of McCarthy's House Un-American Activities Committee.) Burke's anecdote functions as a folksy deflection of the charge of megalomania made against a Blake or a Harold Bloom. It also suggests the tendency going all through Burke's corpus to consider phenomena always in terms of the system they serve or recommend: this is what Burke calls 'motive'.

19

The term motive connotes activity in a way that, say, context does not. We can follow such connotations by looking at three exhibits, two of them from early on in his *Grammar of Motives* (1945). In a section there headed 'Contextual definition' Burke cites Spinoza, who

> explicitly held that all definition is 'negation', which is another way of saying that to define a thing in terms of its context, we must define it in terms of what it is not. And with scholastic succinctness, he formulated the paradox of contextual definition in four words: 'all determination is negation; *omnis determinatio est negatio.*' Since determined things are 'positive', we might point up the paradox as harshly as possible by translating it, 'Every positive is negative'.
>
> (*GM* 25)

Such a harsh translation – every yes a no – is of course regularly performed by Freud; the passage is also a small instance of a large claim, for knowledge being dialectical.

As is suggested by the anecdote with which we began, Burke's love of paradox is not opportunistic but is itself motivated by a thoroughgoing antinomianism. Thus in our second exhibit, the preface to his first published book (1931), Burke explains why he entitled it *Counter-Statement*:

> because – as regards its basic concerns and tenets – each principle it advocates is matched by an opposite principle flourishing and triumphant today. Heresies and orthodoxies will always be changing places, but whatever the minority view happens to be at any given time, one must consider it as 'counter'. Hence the title – which will not, we hope, suggest either an eagerness for the fray or a sense of defeat.
>
> (*CS* vii)

This frankly states the paradox of 'radicalism' or of the oppositional stance as attitude rather than stance; but by stressing the stating rather than the countering we could see the book as counter-*statement*; that is, as setting itself against the constatives

of received meaning and preparing rather for the theory of
language to have been worked out in the so-far-incomplete
trilogy *On Human Relations* in the fifties. Thus *Counter-Statement*,
still much preoccupied with the 'art-for-art's-sake' claims of the
1890s,

> should serve to elucidate a point of view. This point of
> view is somewhat apologetic, negativistic, and even anti-
> nomian, as regards everything but art. It is not antinomian
> as regards art because of a feeling that art is naturally
> antinomian.
>
> (*CS* viii)

Later we are offered the slogan, 'When in Rome, do as the
Greeks' (*CS* 119): what saves this from posturing is Burke's
conviction that there is something systematic always there to be
understood, or to be imposed. His 'Program' extrapolates an
aesthetic attitude (essays on Flaubert, Pater and Gourmont and
on Mann and Gide) to a political attitude – 'attitude' being for
Burke that which motivates form. Scornful of 'historical
relativism' Burke explains 'art for art's sake' not as an escape
from utilitarianism but as its necessary corollary: art is both
corrective and subversive; it is indeed corrective by its subver-
siveness. /

We shall return to the way that Burke's writings continue to
function as an aesthetic, and continue too to demonstrate a
hermeneutic which has powerful applications to literary texts
but our third exhibit, which is again from early in *A Grammar of
Motives*, raises a recurrent methodological problem. Contexts
define, we have been told, and such definition is always negation. Granting this might mean granting the implication that the
work of interpretation is always at an end when this negation
has been revealed. In the parodic 'Prologue in heaven' which
concludes *The Rhetoric of Religion* (1961) the Lord is given as a tic
of speech the demurral 'It's not as simple as that'. To do justice
to any rhetorical situation involves identifying the competing
interests in play – involves identifying them in both senses, of
describing them and of showing how they co-operate. To understand all is to forgive all. Describing this procedure in the
abstract should have shown what the problem with it is. The

21

Grammar is about the 'ratios' of such interests. It begins in a lengthy discussion of 'substance', that on which acts 'stand'. Burke shows how to appeal to 'substance' (or 'principles' or 'first causes') is to gesture towards something that cannot be defined: in poetic terms such appeals might be relished as ambiguity, but in most other terms they look like incoherence. Burke wants to cover both cases with the term 'paradox of substance'. He ends a brief section headed 'The rhetoric of substance' with another 'representative anecdote':

> a list of citizens' signatures had been collected for a petition asking that a certain politician's name be placed on the ballot. In court it was shown that some of these signatures were genuine, but that a great many others were false. Thereupon the judge invalidated the lot on the grounds that, the whole list being a mixture of the false and the genuine, it was 'saturated' with fraud. He here ruled in effect that the list was substantially or essentially fraudulent. The judgement was reversed by a higher court which ruled that, since the required number of genuine signatures had been obtained, the false signatures should be simply ignored. That is, the genuine signatures should be considered in themselves, not contextually.
>
> (*GM* 53)

The problem here is *what* this anecdote represents. The two legal judgements show that 'substance' ('grounds', 'principle') can justify contextual and non-contextual versions of interpretation. But which court is in the right? Burke offers us no hint, and the anecdote serves only to repeat the seeming incoherence of the judgements and thus of the criteria (the 'substance') appealed to in making them. 'Substance', which is that which is held to underlie and to ground the relativism of context, is itself relative to context. We are back to regretting the incoherence, or to relishing the ambiguity. To ask what the anecdote *is* would be the same as asking what it *does*. What difference does it make? The only difference would be in the superiority of the interpreter to either of the competing parties, each of whom would presumably feel that they had got the right result when the judgement favoured them. In other words, the anecdote seems to serve only to reinscribe the 'paradox of substance' and, by extension, to show that propositions and their negations are *in effect* the same thing. That effect seems wholly independent of, and prior to, what the interpretation can do. The end of the heavyweight hermeneutics would be a lightweight pragmatism, a prayer: 'help me to accept – and even celebrate – those things which I cannot change.' It may be that the end of interpretation is always in something banal or tautologous like this. It may be that it is only contingent variations of context, the way the parties line up differently for any interpretative act, that saves any but the simplest of such acts from this banality or tautology. But this is not what Burke would claim. He would claim instead that the act of interpretation is *not* relative. These however would not be his terms. In his own universalizing vocabulary his claim would be that it is in the adaptations to contingent circumstances by an invariant or essential principle – the human body itself, man as 'the symbol-using animal' – that the interpretative work needs to be done. He would deny a determining role to history, which is too weakly relativist an interpreter. Here my argument is with Burke rather than his interpreters, an argument that will run through this book; but, having taken opportunistically some exhibits from the most 'systematic' of his works – a work which for Lentricchia 'is full-blown structuralism' *avant la lettre* (Lentricchia 1983: 67) – I need to contextualize these exhibits. Burke entitles his 1966 collection of essays *Language as Symbolic Action*, a title which summarizes the big system he will call 'Dramatism'.

The introduction to *A Grammar of Motives* (1945) offers Burke's 'pentad'. This is the set of 'five key terms of dramatism' – act, scene, agent, agency, purpose – which correspond respectively to the what, the where and when, the who, the how and the why of all utterances. Utterances are therefore conceived of as 'acts', and most are to be accounted for by a 'ratio' of two of these terms. They are 'acts' in a special sense. In allowing that his five terms are like Kantian categories, Burke also wants to make a distinction: 'Instead of calling them the necessary "forms of experience" ... we should call them the necessary "forms of *talk about* experience" ', the goal of which is 'to temper the absurd ambitions that have their source in faulty terminologies' (*GM* 317). The last part of this remark is an example of the 'neo-liberal ideal' of 'encouraging tolerance by speculation' (*GM* 442) but it is the careful distinction of 'experience' from 'talk about experience' that is relevant here. To paraphrase this as 'language' versus 'meta-language' would be to lose this distinction; in Burke's more usual terms the distinction is between 'action' and 'symbolic action'. William C. Dowling has a nice example:

> to employ Burke's own stress-shifting technique, the paradoxical fact is that a text is both a symbolic *act* and a *symbolic* act: that is, it is a genuine act in that it tries to do something to the world, and yet it is 'merely' symbolic in the sense that it leaves the world untouched.... If, having gotten into an argument in a bar in the rough part of town, I enforce my contempt for someone else's point by making an obscene gesture ... my act remains 'merely' symbolic in that it stands in harmlessly for having punched my adversary in the nose. And yet my gesture is a genuine act nonetheless, or there would be no danger, as there palpably is, of getting my own nose punched in return.
>
> (Dowling 1984: 122)

Famously – or as famous as Burke gets – 'the symbolic act is the *dancing of an attitude*' (*PLF* 9), and an 'attitude' is an 'incipient act' (*RM* 24, 42). Fundamentally for Burke an act is voluntary, and is thus distinguished from a reflex or an event as well as from all those natural phenomena Burke calls '(nonsymbolic) motion' – it is these last which insurance companies categorize as 'acts of God'. Here is Burke on that fundamental:

> the basic unit of action is the human body in purposive motion. We have here a kind of 'lowest common denominator' of action, a minimal requirement that should appear in every act, however many more and greater are the attributes of a complex act.
>
> (*GM* 61)

This will later be codified as a universal dualism: non-symbolic motion versus symbolic action. Here it leads by analogy to the contention that all language, whether as speech-act or as written text, is transitive, instrumental. Language is always, or always potentially, dialogue. Hence Burke returns again and again to drama as a form, most crucially in the long title-essay of *The Philosophy of Literary Form* (1941). We can see the way the analogy works. The body moves to and from something, performs some action which, in however small a way, changes the world. The problem of the analogy is evident however. The gleeful reduction to a 'lowest common denominator' of the body itself leaves out of account the necessity within symbolic actions for a receiver as well as transmitter of symbols: in short for a system, society or economy which would guarantee their efficacy and could decode them. (We might want to argue that even bodily 'acts' require as a minimum some material upon which to work.) In other words, Burke's ambitions for a form of analysis which would not be merely retrospective and pragmatic betrays him into the kind of account of origins (or 'lowest common denominators') found within the systems whose 'grounds' he deconstructs in the same book. In allowing only a binary distinction of 'experience' and 'talk about experience' Burke is implicitly led towards a third term, a meta-linguistic rider that would go, 'all utterances are rhetorical [*except this one*]'. If this sounds like the kind of hostile paradox with which deconstruction was taxed in dozens of journal articles in the 1970s it is as well to be reminded that Burke's founding gesture *is* a gesture, an act. Jameson cites the proclamation in Goethe's *Faust*, 'Im Anfang war die Tat', 'in the beginning was the deed': 'this place of emergence is that of praxis or, in other words, of a unity in which subject and object, thing and language, context and projected action are still at one in the wholeness of a unique gesture' (Jameson 1978: 513). Jameson's idealist language here is not sure if it is yearning for a prelapsarian 'origin' or for the utopia he insists that Marxism must posit, which is at least in keeping with the dichotomy of system and analysis, of prescription and description, which I have just sketched in Burke. He wants his rhetoric to be both.

Burke's insistence on the intentionality of rhetoric – it is the cause in a cause-and-effect model – and thereby on its function as persuasion is of course in line with definitions of rhetoric from the earliest manuals onwards. In his *Rhetoric of Motives* (1950) Burke adds to the traditional sense of rhetoric as persuasion the sense that it is 'inducement to action' (*RM* 50). Near the beginning of that book Burke can describe a quotation from Milton as rhetorical because 'It occurs in a work with a definite audience in mind, and for a definite purpose. It was literature for *use*. Today, it would be called "propaganda" ' (*RM* 4). The word 'propaganda' of course bears peculiar scars from the debates of the thirties and forties; and in this instance Burke is describing a polemically discursive text (Milton's *Areopagitica*), but similar claims are made about poems *in* the thirties. I am thinking of those moments in 'The philosophy of literary form' when, in appearing to seek rapprochement with the New Critics, Burke actually measures his distance from them. For instance, he says there that discussions of 'form' and 'content' can be subsumed under a critical pragmatism which 'assumes that a poem's structure is to be described most accurately by thinking always of the poem's function' (*PLF* 89). What's left implicit in such an assumption is that 'function' needs to be distinguished from both a formalist and a historicist account of it (*CS* 77–81; *RM* 28). This implication would lead us to read the very start of that essay differently: 'Critical and imaginative works are answers to questions posed by the situation in which they arose. They are not merely answers, they are *strategic* answers, *stylized* answers' (*PLF* 1). 'Strategies' there are clearly determined by context rather than being metaphysical acts. Questions posed by the situation in which the poem arose are 'outside' the poem but arise within it, and are opposed to the celebratory tautologies implied by a view of the poem as verbal icon or as well-wrought urn. Later this can become an explicitly historicizing argument. Bourgeois readings could set aside the 'propagandistic ingredient' of historical texts. With the war however it becomes evident that even the work of artists who would invoke for themselves a doctrine of art-for-art's-sake becomes consciously political. The observation leads to this programme:

> One can readily become so involved in such controversies on their own terms, that one neglects to place them in terms of their underlying grammatical principles. What is needed is not that we place ourselves 'above' the controversies. Rather, we should place ourselves *within* them, by an understanding of their essential grammar.
>
> (*GM* 268)

Calling for a 'grammatical' placing of contingent arguments is not, I think, to call for a universalizing rhetoric; instead, the imperative to 'place ourselves *within*' contingent arguments entails interpreting them as production and as action rather than as reproduction and as reaction. (We shall see in the next chapter that Jameson's insistence that interpretation work with 'subtexts' rather than 'contexts' is similar.) Thus rhetoric, though it may be a finite set of strategies and tropes, is available for 'use': 'use' being the particular requirements of agents in particular, contingent circumstances.

This is however a rather cheerful view of agency and of action. Burke's Dramatism depends, as both Jameson and Lentricchia point out, on a conception of the subject as a freely willing and choosing agent. Acts are human acts – even, or especially, when they are scripted. Acts are performed in a realm of Kantian 'freedom'. Burke does not begin, as Locke does or as Marx does, with a transformation of material as the founding act. There is however a shift from the exuberant system-building of *A Grammar of Motives* to the *Rhetoric of Motives*, published five years later, which more nearly aligns itself with the traditional study of rhetoric. Among other things the *Grammar* offers nothing less than a history of philosophy in terms of Burke's Dramatistic pentad of scene, act, agent, agency and purpose. Philosophy is reduced to five species, each under the sign of one of these terms: materialism under scene, idealism under agent, mysticism under purpose, realism under act and pragmatism under agency. (Nominalism and rationalism derive from these.) The exuberance is possible at least in part because of the cheerfully inclusive definition of rhetoric sketched in the introduction, where rhetoric is held to be an appropriate designation for the book's concerns because 'the basic stratagems which people employ ... for the outwitting or cajoling of one another ... all had a "you and me" quality about them' (*GM* xvii). 'You and me' and not, for example, 'them and me' or 'it and me'. By the time of publication of the *Rhetoric* war has been followed by cold war and Burke sees not face-to-face but through a glass darkly. The *Rhetoric* deals, he says,

> with the possibilities of classification in its *partisan* aspects;
> it considers the ways in which individuals are at odds with

one another, or become identified with groups more or less at odds with one another…. Rhetoric is concerned with the state of Babel after the Fall. Its contribution to a 'sociology of knowledge' must often carry us far into the lugubrious regions of malice and the lie.

(*RM* 22–3)

The quotation marks around 'sociology of knowledge' bespeak an uncharacteristic nervousness; not, I suspect, because of any shyness on Burke's part about his competence for such a specialized discourse, more likely as an ironic device distancing himself from a field of study which looked like a front for Marxism.

The ambitions and the dangers inherent in such a concern can perhaps be best discussed by focusing here on an area in which rhetoric has been held to be on safe, because restricted, ground; that is, on rhetoric as a hermeneutic tool in interpreting literary texts. Burke is much more than a literary critic but in an interview given in Winter 1980–1 he acknowledges how much of his later work is 'already there in germ' in the first, most 'aesthetic' book, *Counter-Statement*:

I started from poetry and drama whereas most of such speculation starts from questions of truth and falsity, problems of knowledge. I started with other words for beauty. The first word I threw out was beauty; but I have my equivalents, involving strategies designed to induce cooperation.

(C-G 22)

This shift from intrinsic to extrinsic interpretation suggests a rationale for the translations, the transformations by analogy which characterize Burke's writing and account for its apparent difficulty, its idiosyncracy. Finding the literary text institutionally separate, exiled from where it ought to belong – as cultural criticism, amongst the social sciences – there is a tendency to, as it were, decorate your exile. We seem to be back to Eliot's casting the benighted intellectual as Robinson Crusoe. Yet of course the division of cultural from political power to which Eliot urbanely alludes itself depends on a kind of repression. This can be demonstrated in terms of his own example of *Robinson Crusoe*.

You will remember that Crusoe's careful keeping of dates reveals that, leaving home during the First Civil War, he sits out the whole of the Commonwealth period and the Restoration, returning home just in time for the Glorious Revolution and the re-establishment of a Protestant monarchy – or rather the text does *not* reveal these incidents, about which it is silent. The events of Crusoe's narrative are of his own encounters with matter, colony and economy which unfold as versions of Providence. If the text cannot be said to allude to these other events, I think they can be said to be its unconscious.

I have offered my own example because Burke's essays on literary texts – with the exception of essays on the work of friends like Theodore Roethke, Marianne Moore and William Carlos Williams – are themselves strategic readings, opportunistic if you will. Burke's celebrated essay of 1943 on Keats's 'Ode on a Grecian Urn' which is reprinted as an appendix to the *Grammar of Motives* (GM 447–63) is no exception. Despite its typically bold substitutions ('art' and 'science' for 'beauty' and 'truth'), the essay seems to be determined by the discourse of the New Critics: it trumps their desire for unity by extrapolating from the poem a unity they would never have dreamed of. (For Jameson, Burke's stopping short of what may be implied by his own discovery, or translation of a 'subtext' demonstrates a 'strategy of containment'.) It is, at any rate, too determined by motives ending deftly in the history of ideas to provide an imitable hermeneutic (or an imitable angle on Keats). To regard Burke as exemplary is not the same as regarding him as imitable or as definitive. The claim for exemplariness will be made with an example, but first we may need to remind ourselves that Burke's writings have their own history.

Since *Language as Symbolic Action* (1966) only two lectures, published as *Dramatism and Development* (1972), have appeared as a new book by Burke, but he has continued in essays, polemics and interviews, and in new introductions to their republished editions to expound and extend his systematizing writings of the thirties through the fifties. Much of this has retrospectively defined the founding terms of those writings, revising but never rejecting them. Nor has Burke abstracted his 'system' into some extra-linguistic (or Platonic) realm. His writing is exemplary in the sense that it is what it does. If this means that his writings have not travelled as they might, it means also that they remain active. Cary Nelson argues against paraphrasing Burke, against using his writings as a 'tool-kit' or 'renarrativizing' their insights. He does so in the course of an acute essay mainly on the 'post-systematic' or 'logological' Burke since *The Rhetoric of Religion*:

> Since Burke's major terms have received elaborate explanation in his earlier work, it is now possible for him to use them in a particularly condensed, rhetorical, and, I think, dramatistic way.... As a result Burke's project is pulled in two directions, one holistic and encyclopedic, one comic and self-critical. The terms, in short, at once suggest a total coherent system and a mere series of substitutions, a chain of metonymic displacements in the fragmentary rhetoric of the essays.
>
> (Nelson 1989: 164)

This fine account reminds us that rhetoric cannot be a stable object for interpretation, that there cannot be a metalanguage which is not itself rhetorical. In restricting examples of the gains to be had from Burke's kind of interpretation to canonical literary texts I stressed that this was a provisional restriction. Burke's texts provide us with a model for interpretation, but this does not mean that they forgo their status as objects of interpretation. Use, contingency, context and subtext: these are all terms which describe texts functionally, but functional descriptions are not alternatives to some more restricted, or purer description. Isolating a text restricts one sort of context in favour of another. If we accept a division of Burke's writings into 'Dramatistic' and 'logological' phases or, by extension from Nelson's argument, into system-building and deconstructive phases, or even into books until 1961 and essays since, we may too easily presuppose that 'elaborate explanation' has stabilized or even reified the earlier writings into a set of categories to be placed against texts as though neither were unproblematic. This is why I have not separated an account of Burke's 'system' from an account of some of its implications and some of the problems it raises. I am interested in the exploitation of Burke's 'strategies' rather than the exposition of his 'system' and I want now to try and ground my own claims for the strategic gains to be made through Burke's rhetoric simply by describing a polemical instance of it.

My description is of a brief, proto-structuralist essay which appeared in *Direction* in 1938 and is reprinted in *The Philosophy of Literary Form* (1941). It's called 'Literature as equipment for living'. The title is of course a parody of self-help (or 'Personal Growth') manuals like the one Burke cites as 'How to buy friends and bamboozle oneself and other people'. There's a similar parodic intent in J. L. Austin's *How to Do Things with Words*; but the comparison goes further than that. Burke begins with proverbs, which are what he (and Austin) will call 'acts'. In proverbs

> there is no 'pure' literature.... Everything is 'medicine'. Proverbs are designed for consolation or vengeance, for admonition or exhortation, for foretelling.
>
> Or they name typical, recurrent situations ... [which] are ... developed ... because the names imply a command (what to expect, what to look out for).
>
> (*PLF* 293–4)

Then comes the typical analogical turn, to the question, 'could the most complex and sophisticated works of art legitimately be considered somewhat as "proverbs writ large"?' (*PLF* 296); then the programme for a sociological criticism, requiring 'active categories' that could account for the proverb and for the literary text as action (*PLF* 296, 303), and would be inclusive rather than exclusive. Each proverb is a *strategy*, a word Burke defends at length (*PLF* 297–300). He likes the word partly for its military provenance (so the epigraph to the *Grammar of Motives* is *ad bellum purificandum*, 'to purify warfare', and central to *The Rhetoric of Religion* is a notion of logomachy, 'the War of Words'). Though he doesn't use the term 'rhetoric' here, Burke is describing rhetoric as a set of strategies. The work of art is 'the strategic naming of a situation' (*PLF* 300) and, in another surprising yoking by analogy, slang too is the result of new situations needing new names.

Two things give Burke pause. The first is something we have already noted, the preservation of a category of essence. Here Burke claims that 'fables name an "essence" ': the fact that fables or proverbs can be applied to all sorts of irreproducible circumstances presupposes an 'essence' of those circumstances. Proverbs 'are, like philosophy, sufficiently "generalized" to extend far beyond the particular combination of events named by them in any one instance' (*PLF* 301). The quotation marks Burke puts around the words 'generalized' and 'essence' indicate the embarrassment this admits into such a bravura piece. The bravura returns however in his pre-emptive response to the second qualification. Burke responds to the kind of criticism which was to be levelled against structuralist readings, as well as to his own rhetoric as it is exemplified here. Such a rhetoric

> might occasionally lead us to outrage good taste, as we sometimes found exemplified in some great sermon or tragedy or abstruse work of philosophy the same strategy as we found exemplified in a dirty joke. At this point, we'd put the sermon and the dirty joke together, thus 'grouping by situation' and showing the range of possible particularizations. In his exceptionally discerning essay, 'A Critic's Job of Work', R. P. Blackmur says, 'I think on the whole his (Burke's) method could be applied with equal fruitfulness to Shakespeare, Dashiell Hammett, or Marie Corelli'. When I got through wincing, I had to admit that Blackmur was right. This article is an attempt to say for the method what can be said. As a matter of fact, I'll go a step further and maintain: You can't properly put Marie Corelli and Shakespeare apart until you have first put them together. First genus, then differentia.
>
> (*PLF* 302)

As the last aphorism here suggests, the analogical categories Burke is drawn to may be those of biology and not sociology. The piece ends however with Burke's recommendation of 'sociological categories' in which rhetoric would be 'active' like the phenomena it categorizes. Such categories

> would consider works of art ... as strategies for selecting enemies and allies, for socializing losses, for warding off evil eye, for purification, propitiation, and desanctification, consolation and vengeance, admonition and

exhortation, implicit commands or instructions of one sort or another.

(*PLF* 304)

Furthermore these categories would attempt to be inclusive rather than exclusive by classifying according to invariant, shared factors rather than according to particular variations. Ways by which the latter can be classified are almost infinite – 'Apples can be grouped with bananas as fruits, and they can be grouped with tennis balls as round' (*PLF* 303) – and Burke claims that his method can supersede any such exclusive taxonomy with 'a reintegrative point of view, a broader empire of investigation encompassing the lot' (*PLF* 304). Though he delightedly refers to the likelihood that such a procedure will scandalize 'those persons who take the division of faculties in our universities to be an exact replica of the way in which God himself divided up the universe' (*PLF* 303), two paradoxes arising from this claim are not referred to. First, the charge of idiosyncracy, of 'intuitive leaps', is addressed but not answered: what is 'implicit' to one interpreter may remain invisible to another. Second, the inclusiveness depends on a reduction – on reducing social and literary phenomena to a strategy (or essence) which is irreducible – and what is put together in this way may not subsequently be put apart in a way that does justice to its particular use.

I have used the 'Literature as equipment for living' essay to try and show both the virtues and limitations of Burke's rhetoric. If, like Robinson Crusoe, we're concerned with keeping the books, some debits need to be entered. First, Burke seems to have preferred his 'wild man' role to engaging with work which would bear directly on his project: most glaringly, he has until recently ignored Saussure, whose work is surely germane to the whole 'Motives' project. Likewise with Wittgenstein, and with speech-act theory. Second, Burke's suspicion of anything that smacks of determinism leads him to cling to the notion that figuration is grounded in the language user and not in the language. There is then a sort of nostalgia for the subject, connected to a liberal piety which, we shall see, Burke can attack in theory while continuing to rely on it in practice – the piety that to debunk or to demystify something will render it powerless.

(Burke insists, it must be said, that the rhetorical resources of language users are possessed by a community, whose competing interests are always acknowledged.) Third, what I have here taken as central, Burke's notion of rhetoric as action or as 'inducement to action', of course begs the question, what action? So what? I find Lentricchia's answer too optimistic, too smug in its role of left humanist and I suspect that Burke's mere (or merely fictive) refusal to acknowledge a separation of literary power from social power simply cannot prove exemplary – though it may prove talismanic. What is exemplary, I think, is the notion of rhetoric (of knowledge) as a conflict rather than a conversation in another representative anecdote from 'The philosophy of literary form':

> Imagine that you enter a parlor. You come late. When you arrive, others have long preceded you, and they are engaged in a heated discussion, a discussion too heated for them to pause and tell you exactly what it is about. In fact, the discussion had already begun long before any of them got there, so that no one present is qualified to retrace for you all the steps that had gone before. You listen for a while, until you decide that you have caught the tenor of the argument; then you put in your oar. Someone answers; you answer him; another comes to your defense; another aligns himself against you, to either the embarrassment or gratification of your opponent, depending upon the quality of your ally's assistance. However, the discussion is interminable. The hour grows late, you must depart. And you do depart, with the discussion still vigorously in progress.
>
> (PLF 110–11)

This is a representation of history both as without contingency (the living and the dead argue in the same room) and as only contingency (one more voice is added, then departs). It is a useful symbol for the manifold of Burke's project since it not only summarizes but also problematizes that project. This is great matter in a little room. It summarizes some topics – drama, 'grounds', history and rhetoric themselves – which will be the subject of the next chapter.

2

A god coming down to earth

For Burke, things move, people act, and 'man is the symbol-using animal' (*LSA* 53, 3).[1] Rhetoric, the deployment and exchange of symbols, is the definitively human activity. Thus the first paragraph of *A Grammar of Motives*: 'The book is concerned with the basic forms of thought which, in accordance with the nature of the world as all men necessarily experience it, are exemplified in the attributing of motives' (*GM* xv). We may react to the all-inclusive ambitions of such a statement by baulking at the coerciveness of its terms – basic, all, necessarily. Yet the Kantian ambitiousness of such a programme also does little more than to take the linguistic turn of twentieth-century philosophy out into (as they say) left field. In talking about morality, or art, or God, we are talking about language. From as early as *Counter-Statement* (1931) a similarly essentialist appeal is made for the categorization of this necessary experience:

> The universal experiences are implicated in specific modes of experience: they arise out of the relationship between the organism and its environment.... The same universal experience could invariably accompany the same mode of experience only if all men's modes of experience were identical.
>
> (*CS* 150)

A statement like this implicitly contains much else that is important in Burke's project. Lentricchia can found his argument largely on *Counter-Statement* without anachronism because so much of the whole project is incipient in Burke's first book.

35

Burke describes practices which tend to be redescribed and elaborated rather than qualified or retracted later. Indeed, redescription and elaboration are themselves practices for which a rationale is sketched here. This statement is a kind of summary before the fact of a context-dependent theory of interpretation. Such a theory is prey to a charge that it is relativist or weakly pragmatist but, given the absolute premise (there are 'universal experiences'), the rest follows logically enough. As Burke will also point out however, it may follow logically and not temporally: conclusions may 'follow' from premises that are derived after them. The statement also stands as a summary before the fact of the substitutions and translations which will characterize Burke's project. In this chapter, for instance, we shall consider his stress on the practice of secularizing religious terms (demystification), and on the seemingly contrary practice, the process of mystification. The first half of this chapter is concerned with Burke's argument with 'Historicism', the second with the implications this has for his interpretative practice. But our first instance will be Burke's stress on terms drawn from drama for what he here calls 'experience', and his claim that those terms describe human action literally rather than metaphorically.

The work of the thirties is much concerned with 'form' as a function of the rhetorical exchanges between the work and its reader or audience. Textual effects cannot be unitary, nor can ideology be monolithic: 'there are no forms of art which are not forms of experience outside of art' (CS 143). Descriptions of 'art' in terms of 'act' will have as much justification as the much commoner description of 'art' in terms of 'experience'. For this reason it is pre-eminently drama which reveals the homology of 'art' and 'experience'. In the postscript (dated January 1953) to the second edition of Counter-Statement Burke writes that all his books to that point

> take their start from a principle of form typified in drama. This principle was capable of development with regard to the non-verbal situations in which such expression takes place. Since 'symbolic action' really is a kind of action empirically observable, the author contends that a terminology thus developed in conformity with the forms of drama is not the sheer use of analogy, the extended

36

ramifying of a metaphor, but is strictly literal in reference. Man *is* the specifically symbol-using animal, and a 'Dramatistic' theory of motives is systematically grounded in this view of human essence.

(*CS* 219)

Drama can name and embody the participants of verbal conflicts, but it is not the case that a set of terms drawn from either has priority. They cannot be distinguished. Similarly, Burke appeals to the secular etymology of theological terms like grace, create and spirit, to show that their crossing-over is not a unique, one-way event:

> For whereas the words for the 'supernatural' realm are necessarily borrowed from the realm of our everyday experiences, out of which our familiarity with language arises, once a terminology has been developed for special theological purposes the order can become reversed. We can borrow back the terms from the borrower, again secularizing to varying degrees the originally secular terms that had been given 'supernatural' connotations.

(*RR* 7)

In calling the system he elaborates through the 1940s and 1950s 'Dramatism' then, Burke admits a continuity between acting on the stage and in the world. Although Burke calls what he is doing in *The Rhetoric of Religion* and subsequently 'Logology', this rests on the same principle as the earlier work: we live *in* symbols as well as *by* them. Hence metaphor is a means of direction, of motivation, rather than an adjunct or a metalanguage. The reflexive function of language, its capacity to use words about words, is what is distinctively human about it. The most fundamental of Burke's apparent metaphors for such distinctiveness is stabilized by the assertion that it is literal:

> man is defined literally as an animal characterized by his special aptitude for 'symbolic action' which is itself a literal term. And from there on, drama is employed, not as a metaphor but as a fixed form that helps us discover what the implications of the terms 'act' and 'person' *really* are.

37

Once we choose a generalized term for what people do, it is certainly as literal to say that 'people act' as it is to say that they 'but move like mere things'.

(D 448)[2]

This is a principle from which a methodology of interpretation can be derived. It is a consistent principle, but by no means without its problems. For example, neither the shift of terms from 'symbolic action' to 'act' and 'person' nor the assertion that interpretation must discover the implications of those terms follows from it straightforwardly. No matter how elaborate a system of classification or of interpretation it still depends on the objects it classifies or interprets. As Burke writes in the addendum to the third edition of *Counter-Statement*, 'the modes of rhetorical appeal can be stated in highly *generalized* terms, yet any given exhortation arises out of a context so immediately urgent as to be unique' (*CS* 224). The question of what actions are to be the object of analysis can then be answered with a shrug: whatever comes to hand. (Compare Burke's dictum that 'the main ideal of criticism ... is to use all that there is to use', *PLF* 23.) This is one import, as we have seen, of the representative anecdote quoted at the end of Chapter 1.

The anecdote occurs in the midst of a lengthy section of 'The philosophy of literary form' essay (1941) entitled 'Ritual drama as hub'. The section begins by assuming that 'the social sphere', consisting of 'situations and acts', can be dealt with as a drama, while 'the physical sphere' of mere events needs to be 'considered in mechanistic terms' (*PLF* 103). Thus the description of 'scene' belongs to the physical sciences, that of 'acts' belongs to the social sciences (*PLF* 114). Ritual drama is taken as the 'hub' or Ur-form of drama. It does not matter to Burke whether its priority is temporal or not – it can be seen as culmination or as unsurpassable precursor of all drama. It can also be very broadly defined, so as to include Plato's dialectic for example. Indeed, though the section begins by discussing *Hamlet* and ends with a 'satyr-play' of Burke's own, there is little reference to plays. Burke is concerned with the *form* of drama as a ritual for purification, as the response to a situation. Characteristically, the 'ritual drama' discussed at most length is a representative anecdote. This one concerns a writer who writes, then binges on alcohol. The inference made is that the successive, discrete phases are in effect simultaneous, mutually entailing. The writing and the drinking are alike 'conjurings', better seen as respectively spiritual and material versions of the same power than as its benign and malign phases.

If I have fairly summarized this anecdote, and its function, in the end it is tautologous, or banal. I think though that it is a serious banality, which can be approached by way of a later (1965) summarizing comment about drama:

> If *action* is to be our key term, then *drama*; for drama is the culminative form of action.... But if *drama*, then *conflict*. And if *conflict*, then *victimage*. Dramatism is always on the edge of this vexing problem, that comes to a culmination in the song of the scapegoat.
>
> (*LSA* 54–5)

Drama entails a kind of ritual embodiment (in the figure of the scapegoat); this may be ritual however not only in the sense of stylized communal action but also in the sense of merely routine action. This paradox in Burke has attracted Geoffrey Hartman, who says 'Burke sets purgation against purification'; but the question of a 'pure' deconstructed discourse for Hartman 'goes right through this problem of ideology to that of theology' (Hartman 1980: 93, 111). Burke's movement towards theology is indeed one that will need to be considered, but I want to draw a secular as well as a theological lesson from the anecdote in the last paragraph. In secular terms, Burke is fond of citing Coleridge's dictum, 'extremes meet'. This gives him licence for the kind of interpretative *fiat* I have already described as Freud's 'Every yes a no' – as in Burke's advice, 'wherever you find a doctrine of "nonpolitical" esthetics affirmed with fervor, look for its politics' (*RM* 28). There is though, as I have said, a second, 'theological' inference. In wanting to remain unillusioned about the claims for confession as purgation made both by psycho-analysis and religion, Burke is left with tautology. Changes in the world are only apparent. 'Ritual drama as hub' closes, beyond all this fiddle, with a fable, 'Electioneering in psychoanalysia', in which the changes wrought by democratic succession are only changes of figurehead. The son replaces the father, then becomes the scapegoat next time around, but all the time actual power resides with the uncles: 'Hence, nothing is changed. Hence, since all the ills survive intact, there is nothing to do the following year but repeat the mummery all over again, thereby getting a *sense* of relief and promise and newness' (*PLF* 136). Burke has been explicit that the fable allegorizes pessimism specifically about American democracy. The seriousness of the tautology arises however from the inference that drama is about conflicts which are *only* ritualistic. If Burke can be eclectic, even cavalier, about the materials offered for Dramatistic analysis, there is less room for bravado about its results:

> If we enact by tragedy a purificatory ritual symbolizing our enrollment in a cause shaped to handle a situation accurately … we may embody the same processes as if we enacted a purificatory ritual symbolizing our enrollment in a cause woefully inadequate to the situation. And the analyst of the two tragedies may, by reason of his over-all classificatory terms, find much in common between the two symbolic acts. The fact remains, however, that one of these acts embodies a chart of meanings superior to the other (and if the chart is too far out of accord with the nature of the situation, the 'unanswerable opponent', the objective recalcitrance of the situation itself, will put forth its irrefutable rejoinder).
>
> (*PLF* 131)

Here the parenthesis seems to take away what much of the rest of Burke has given us. The 'unanswerable opponent' is a new god-term[3] – compare Aristotle's Unmoved Mover or Fredric Jameson's 'unsurpassable horizon' – implying that in the end drama and our interpretation of it is neither here nor there. In the end. Both the ends of analysis and the principles from which it proceeds (covered by Burke's term 'grounds') will remain a question which, if it is 'unanswerable' must nevertheless be asked. The question is one of temporal as well as logical *priority*, a question inextricable from the issue of historical change.

From his relatively earlier writings Burke is aware that accounting for historical change represents a crucial problem. This is from *Permanence and Change* (1935):

the *rationale* of pre-evolutionary thought, which refuses to consider things in the light of their genesis, is founded on the feeling that, unless you can name the critical points at which qualitative changes take place, your account of derivations is too truncated to be of real service. This would be the basis of a theologian's refusal, for instance, to accept Marxian or psychoanalytic explanations of the genesis of religion.

(PC 143–4)

Here Burke is with the theologians and against Darwin, whose account of variation is, later, seen to be complicit with the liberal and idealist imperatives of nineteenth-century England. (*GM* 152–8). To recognize an increase of complexity is to recognize merely a quantitative change: to be stuck, in Burke's example, with the recognition that water, ice and steam are essentially the same. On the other hand, the problem of identifying 'qualitative transformations' is one that necessarily requires new methodological resources.

One option Burke does not take is to separate a fictively static object of analysis from an account of how it got to be there. This is what Saussure does, for example, in distinguishing a 'synchronic' from a 'diachronic' realm as a preliminary to linguistic analysis. Indeed, though Burke does make similar distinctions (most clearly in *The Rhetoric of Religion*) he assumes that both realms can be dealt with together. In *Attitudes Toward History* (1937) this can result in some breathtaking sweeps of narrative. In a couple of paragraphs Burke accounts for hundreds of years. He claims that between Aquinas (1226–74) and Marx (1818–83) social thought took the part for the whole, the dominant interest-group for 'man' or 'society' and that it turned paradox into orthodoxy, as in Mandeville's 'private vices, publick benefits':

[Adam] Smith proceeds simply by rationalizing Mandeville *without* the paradox; ambition becomes a private virtue because it is a public virtue. The utilitarians completed his theory. Thus, in England, the 'transvaluation of values' had gained codification and authoritative backing long before Nietzsche, in more feudalistic Germany, began to

41

put it forward challengingly and confusedly. And Marx, whose English training had shown him its ascendancy, laid out the formula for its *rejection*.

(*ATH* 24–5)

The genealogy may or may not be convincing, but the point is surely that Burke can opportunistically practise such narrative to exemplify something else (here the 'transvaluation of values').

History is where we are, by telling us how we got here, but its value is prospective, even predictive: 'A history of the past is worthless except as a documented way of talking about the future' (*ATH* 159). Burke offers an account of western history as a five-act drama – a kind of diachronic pentad – which promises nothing less than a history of ideology in sixty pages. This is not of course a promise that can be fulfilled: Act One sees the Roman Empire as supported ideologically by a declining stoicism and an emergent 'Christian heresy' but Act Five is summary, a sketch for a utopia of collectivism which nevertheless ends by 'point[ing] out that the individual is a bondsman who "justifies" himself by paying tribute to the norms of his society' (*ATH* 165). Burke's vocabulary here is heavily inflected by Marx. Writing the book, Burke assumed a 'spiritual impulse' would underlie his account of epochal transition

> but as we proceeded we found the economic emphasis inescapable. For even if you assume that there is some 'spiritual' factor operating at the imperial 'core', the enterprising area from which the whole organization radiates, it still seems that the upbuilding of an empire as a whole can only be explained by economic factors.
>
> (*ATH* 115)

Historically there is typically the reverse of the process Burke describes as having occurred when he wrote the book: spiritual concerns are the vocabulary of co-operation adopted by those who have jumped on the economic bandwagon.

There is an imperative for justification, which is a historical imperative. Once again history is rendered homely, indeed domestic, by Burke's example of the invention of labour-saving devices:

In using such contrivances without having 'earned' them as their inventor did, we may become much like barbarians among monuments of a culture to which they are alien....
We must *earn* an inheritance by taking it as the basis of a new problem.... If we do not ... if we merely squander our inheritance rather than making it the basis of a new 'job', the process of 'alienation' is under way.

(*ATH* 125)

The imperative is a Hegelian one for the incorporation of the past in order to act in the present and to progress into the future, but the example shows that Burke wants the imperative to hold for daily life in the present and prospectively, and not merely for the retrospective business of interpretation. As we saw him say in another, more strictly interpretative context, you can't put these apart without first putting them together.

Such *tours de force* of narrative then may be less characteristic of Burke than the practice of listing, categorizing, putting things in hierarchies. Though he calls for 'active categories' (*PLF* 303), this is basically a 'synchronic' practice, a concern with intrinsic 'forms'. So *Attitudes Toward History* ends with a 'Dictionary of pivotal terms' in which the ambitions for a narrative of history are substituted by the synchrony of an arbitrary, alphabetical order: sixty pages for the 'History', more than double that for the 'Dictionary'. We have seen that *Attitudes Toward History* involves an attitude towards the future in the sense of something that can be brought into being. No-one would call *A Grammar of Motives* unambitious, and one of its ambitions, perhaps, is for a prior accounting of events. *Attitudes Toward History* offers (in part) a diachronic account of human history as a drama or as a collective poem. The *Grammar* offers its history of philosophy synchronically, as a grid of actual and possible relations, so that the question of whether its interpretative grid may be retrospective or predictive does not really arise. As Burke writes of the *Grammar* in 1953, 'here a poor mathematician seeks in his way to attain the generalizing ways of pure mathematics' (*CS* 218). This is a different ambition, not just a different idiom. In one sense it is an irreconcilable difference from the Marxism of the Third International. In another it is the working out of the implications of an interpretative paradox mentioned somewhere by Kierkegaard: our lives are lived forwards, but they are understood backwards.

Language as Symbolic Action begins with a 1963 essay called 'Definition of Man'. The anthropological motive implied by that title is inseparable from a verbal or 'logological' motive which has Burke first defining 'definition'. Definition is a logical starting-point but may temporally have occurred anywhere; a logical or narrative order may not be the same as an actual order of events: 'the first principle may have been the last thing arrived at and hence is "prior" in this purely nontemporal sense of priority' (*LSA* 3). Burke later reiterates this opening, claiming that it is a peculiarly nineteenth-century tendency to assume that logical and temporal priority are actually the same. Hence Poe's famous essay 'The principles of composition', which shows how his poem 'The Raven' was derived from a set of principles, is for Burke a falsification. More likely, Burke suggests, the poem would have derived from a rhythm or from a story, and could only be seen retrospectively to embody such principles. Poe's essay falsifies in the sense that it locates its logical first term (a poetic principle) as the term which occurred first in time. Narrative must falsify events because it is compelled to present them in logical rather than temporal sequence, or rather to confuse logic with temporality:

> It's much as though, when confronting a syllogism such as
> 'All men are mortal, Socrates is a man, therefore Socrates
> is mortal', we were to situate the first premise yesterday,
> the second premise today, and the conclusion tomorrow.
>
> (*LSA* 36)

Burke's impatience with what he calls 'Historicism', then, is with a kind of nineteenth-century historiography, with history as a narrative. The impatience is due to what he sees as the bad faith of history-writing, its concealment of the inductive process by which it posits causes for effects. 'Historicism' for Burke thus represents history as a narrative which conceals its dialectical character, as a narrative which has written itself.

It also tends towards a crude determinism, overvaluing 'scene' at the expense of other terms. As Burke puts this much later in the *All-Area* interview (given in 1980–1 and published in

1983): 'what I call the *historical* heresy, or fallacy, is to see us purely as products of the particular historical period in which we happen to have lived. I have to see us as transforming a universal identity' (C-G 22). This summarizes a consistent interpretative principle but itself omits the stages by which the principle was arrived at. In *Permanence and Change* Burke argues that to replace a dialectic ending in synthesis by one based solely on antagonism can only be retrograde. He is arguing, of course, against Marx, and suggests rewriting the term 'dialectical materialism' as 'dialectical biologism':

> Historic textures can be said to 'cause' our frameworks of interpretation in the sense that they present varying kinds of material for us to synthesise – but the synthesis is necessarily made with reference to non-historic demands, the genius of the human body as projected into its ideological counterparts.
>
> (PC 229)

Marx can be tarred with the same 'historicist' brush as Darwin, as a storyteller who not only has substituted the 'agents' of a story with its 'scene' but also has rearranged its events so that they accord with a logic discerned in interpreting them.

This distinction of temporal from logical sequence – which is, more intuitively, a distrust of placing 'first principles' or 'origins' prior to exemplary situations or 'representative anecdotes' – animates the consideration of 'grounds' in *A Grammar of Motives*. Burke's own 'refusal to consider things in the light of their genesis' must apparently cause problems for a system ambitious to account for all human things. His project does not, at this point, in its most ambitious and comprehensive manifestation, contain its own abstraction or grounding. Burke here furnishes an ethics and an aesthetics without a philosophy of mind. (As Paul Kenny once put it, he has his second and third critiques without the first.) For Burke himself this is a principled omission rather than a lack. He returns again and again to the apparently unarguable premise of the body itself. In the introduction to *A Grammar of Motives* he brings forward his 'five key terms of Dramatism' while refusing to make Dramatism a metaphysics which would subsume all other terms and from which they would all derive. Furthermore, he promises to do so by employing spatial metaphors rather than the temporal metaphors which, as we have seen, entail at best confusion, at worst falsification: thus 'placement' rather than 'historical survey' (*GM* xxii–xxiii).

Initially, what are thus placed are the 'grounds' on which a variety of metaphysicians do erect their systems. As Burke points out, the word 'ground' is itself a scenic term ('We can discern the scenic reference if the question, "On what grounds did he do this?" is translated: "What kind of scene did he say it was, that called for such an act?" ' *GM* 12). We have already noticed that Burke's identifications and descriptions of paradox can leave themselves in what looks like tautology or banality. I want to look at why this should be so in some instance of 'grounds' in Burke, then at his own means of escape from the paradox. Again I take my orientation from Fredric Jameson's essay which sees the limitations and the achievement of Burke's corpus as inextricable, and thus sees a paradox in that corpus itself. Recognizing that 'context' (Burke's 'scene') must itself be a text might, for Jameson, tempt us into mistaken idealism: 'this does not mean that history is itself a text, only that it is inaccessible to us except in textual form, or, in other words, that we approach it only by way of its prior textualization' (1988: 141). Burke is exemplary in offering to cancel this dichotomy; but this very cancellation of differences can leave us with an idealist or textual paradox, in inertia. For Jameson, this can in turn be cancelled by substituting the term 'subtext', an intrinsic category:

> The symbolic act ... begins by producing its own context in the same moment of emergence in which it steps back over against it, measuring it with an eye to its own active project. The whole paradox of what we are calling the subtext can be measured by this, that the literary work or cultural object itself, as though for the first time, brings into being that situation to which it is also at one and the same time a reaction.
>
> (1988: 141)

Burke's willingness not just to account for everything but to *accommodate* everything can lead to this paradox. His refusal of 'historicism' or 'relativism' for instance begs a question: what is it that our analyses, our acts of interpretation, *do*?

In *A Rhetoric of Motives* Burke cites an anthropological example from the earlier *Grammar*. We may say that a tribe living by a river has a 'river god'. In using the term 'god' however, by regarding this practice as superstition or animism, we would idealize: 'gods' may be better understood as 'summarized terms for motives'. Relativism commits the relativist to a position in which to understand all is to forgive all. However, it has been a crucial insight of twentieth-century anthropology that the analyst or spectator is not neutral or invisible. The behaviour she observes may be modified, or may only be taking place at all, because of her presence. What cannot be forgiven then is our own position of power, as anthropologists, in the present. Our acts of analysis have accreted theological meanings, whereas 'even the most theological of terms can be implicitly modified by very accurate nontheological meanings, which, though they may not show through the expression itself, were clearly felt by the persons using it' (*RM* 111).

This is an example of what Burke calls the 'limitations of debunking'. The point is not to debunk, demystify or reduce one set of terms to another. The activity suggested is one in which the idealized and the debunked, like the cause and the effect, can be regarded simultaneously or, to change the metaphor from temporal to spatial, where they can occupy the same space. The point is made again in anthropological terms in the *Grammar*:

> When a weapon or implement or art was said to possess a divine or heroic origin, we would consider this simply as a way of characterizing it as a power or motive in keeping with the terms of definition then available ... [but] we should propose to translate the statement that a certain implement *came from* a power into a statement that this implement was *essentially* a power. That is, we should translate the notion of origin from terms of time to terms of timelessness (terms that consider it *sub specie aeternitatis*).... In sum, a statement that an art was descended from a God would be interpretable as a statement that the art was in itself a power, or motive.
>
> (*GM* 118)

We are urged to consider power without origin, as in an economy rather than in a narrative. Narratives necessarily distort. They must depend on what Burke calls the 'temporizing of essence': 'the *narrative* way of trying to say how things *truly are* is to say how they *originally were*' ((N)M/(S)A 831). Burke's preference for terms like 'essence' and 'timelessness' over terms drawn from a system like economics may seem surprising following, as this does in the *Grammar*, a lengthy discussion of how money has, under capitalism, taken on the symbolic functions of God as 'ground'. If we are surprised, it is not because these terms are opportunistic. Indeed, they recur.

We have seen that in revealing the untenability of certain hierarchic pairs or binary oppositions Burke may be left passive, in a posture of mere pragmatic reaction, of 'prophecy after the event' (*LSA* 81). A subtle means of escape from this bind is suggested. It is represented for example by Burke's summary of Spinoza. A conventional account would run that Spinoza answers the mind–body dualism of Descartes with monism, the mind and body as one. While Burke largely repeats such an account, for him a hierarchy does remain:

> For body but represents itself, whereas mind can represent both body and itself. Or otherwise put, there are bodies, ideas of bodies, and ideas of ideas. Or in Spinoza's terms: 'In God there is necessarily an idea which expresses the essence of this or that human body *sub aeternitas specie*'.
>
> (*GM* 150)

Such moments occur not just for the 'scenic philosopher' – similar moments are identified for example in Kant (*GM* 195). The end of paradox, or its best example, is always mystical: timelessness and essence. Burke's own first terms are from ethics, from acts. His final terms are mystical, just as *Grammar of Motives* ends with the category of 'purpose' which correlates with the philosophy of 'mysticism'. The end of a series which can finally take him outside the disjunction of temporal and logical series lies in theology.

As we have seen, Burke does not separate change from system, nor make the kind of distinction made by Saussure between horizontal movement through time and a vertical sectioning of it. Rather, he wants to separate 'time' from 'essence'. In the opening pages of *The Rhetoric of Religion* he again distinguishes 'time' from 'logic'. Time, a narrative or simply linguistic sequence, requires a 'poetic terminology' while logic, an essence which, though it must be contained in a temporal series, *pervades* that series, requires a 'philosophic terminology'. Thus a quotation from Augustine leads Burke to a related distinction, employing a metaphor not from motion but from mysticism: ' "Time" is to "eternity" as the particulars in the unfolding of a sentence are to the sentence's unitary meaning' (*RR* 23). It would be a little too easy to observe that Burke is following Augustine (the subject of his next chapter) on a route from rhetoric to theology. Rather, theology is the discourse which attempts to provide rhetoric with its ultimate 'ground'. (Another of Burke's terms for 'ground' is 'god-term'.) Burke protests that *The Rhetoric of Religion* is 'concerned not directly with religion, but rather with the *terminology* of religion; not directly with man's relationship to God, but rather with his relationship to the *word* "God" ' (*RR* vi).

Given Burke's 'definition of man', his 'grounds' for human behaviour, it may be disingenuous of him to posit here an extra-linguistic God, a God who is beyond words like the ineffable God of negative theology, another 'unanswerable opponent'. As *The Rhetoric of Religion* demonstrates though, Burke is not content simply to leave such a category in a bin labelled 'things whereof one cannot speak'. It is one of the paradoxes of negative theology that, though God may only be known through an incommunicable revelation, the theology itself is an attempt to communicate this through demonstrating its incommunicability. Furthermore, at points throughout Burke's writing it is suggested that negation itself may be the definitive marker of human language, a suggestion that will be given the full treatment in *Language as Symbolic Action* (419–79). So, although God may be the ultimate 'ground', it needs to be remembered that a logical first term should not be confused with what occurs first in time. By extension, the product of an analysis includes not just the process by which what is analysed has come to be what it is, but the process of the analysis too. (This is what Hegel's dialectic insists upon.) Burke insists that 'grounds' are to be found in 'form' and not vice versa:

When psychologists seek to derive human institutions from the nature of man, rather than deriving the nature of man from his institutions, they are apparently moved by the feeling that ... the pressure of institutions alone could not account for the entire expression. But when they looked for 'priority', they sought it in the 'unconscious-irrational', a psychological source, rather than in the *dialectical*, a formal source. And their rich contribution to the study of symbolism can thus mislead, if it causes us to treat formal logic as merely derivative from psycho-logic.

(*RM* 283)

On this basis Freud can be enlisted as a kind of unconscious dialectician, as a student of the forms of symbolic action rather than of its grounds. The recuperation (or rewriting) of Freud is accomplished by reversing the priority of the terms in what remains a reciprocal relationship. 'Form' for Burke is a system of *acts* rather than an immobile structure and, as such, seeks 'grounds' for its acts. Section VI of 'Definition of Man' sets a notion of perfectibility (Aristotle's 'entelechy') against a notion apparently counter to it, Freud's 'repetition compulsion'. The section concludes thus:

there are sheerly technical reasons, intrinsic to the nature of language, for belief in God and the Devil. Insofar as language is intrinsically hortatory (a medium by which men can attain the cooperation of one another), God perfectly embodies the petition. Similarly, insofar as vituperation is a 'natural' resource of speech, the Devil provides a perfect butt for invective. Heaven and Hell together provide the ultimate, or perfect, grounding for sanctions.

(*LSA* 20)

This extrapolates a principle on which, for example, Burke's rhetorical reading of Hitler's *Mein Kampf* was based (*PLF* 191–220). It is significant here that the end of rhetoric is 'co-operation': with 'communication' this is the desire of the two books most imbrued with the Depression, *Permanence and Change* and *Attitudes Toward History*. In this quotation from the

50

1960s however the theological terms have taken over priority. By this point it seems that to begin in a grounding notion of 'ideology' would be to repeat the mistake of psychology in trying to bypass dialectic.

Ideology is one of the 'traditional principles of rhetoric' listed by Burke in the *Rhetoric of Motives* (101–10). Rhetoric is for him a kind of ideological conflict which is both before and beyond economic divisions. So it becomes a means of putting together Freud and Marx, the body and the body politic. Ideology is also itself something like the 'ground' of all argument. Hence the rhetorical question from 'Definition of Man': 'Do we simply use words, or do they not also use us? An "ideology" is like a god coming down to earth, where it will inhabit a space pervaded by its presence' (*LSA* 6). Such an analogy ascribes to ideology functions which, as we have seen, are ascribed also to 'critical and imaginative works' (*PLF* 1), to the object of analysis which, in Jameson's summary, 'brings into being that situation to which it is also at one and the same time a reaction' (Jameson 1988: 141). The terms of the analogy are also significant in that here ideology performs a theological function. In *Rhetoric of Motives* Burke argues that theology represents rhetoric, so that ' "Eden" and "the Fall" are mythic terms for composition and division' (*RM* 176). He wants to define ideology as functioning more pervasively than is allowed within a crude base–superstructure model. In trying to do so he is led to suggest that just as theology represents rhetoric, so rhetoric must represent theology:

> Ideology cannot be deduced from economic considerations alone. It also derives from man's nature as a 'symbol-using animal'. And since the 'original economic plant' is the human body, with the divisive centrality of its particular nervous system, the theologian's concerns with Eden and the 'fall' come close to the heart of the rhetorical problem. For, behind the theology, there is the perception of generic divisiveness which, being common to all men, is a universal fact about them, prior to any divisiveness caused by social classes. Here is the basis of rhetoric. Out of this emerge the motives for linguistic persuasion. Then, *secondarily*, we get the motives peculiar to particular economic situations.
>
> (*RM* 146)

For Burke, 'social estrangement' must itself only be a version of a prior division, a division between the self and society as motives. Following hard on this recognition comes a recognition of reciprocal 'interest' and a desire to repair the division, the ultimate manifestation of which is religion. This scheme leads Burke to treat 'identification' rather than persuasion as the principle of rhetoric in the first part of *Rhetoric of Motives*. This in turn leads to the notion of 'courtship', later defined (with a nod to William Empson) as 'the use of suasive devices for the transcending of social estrangement' (*RM* 208).

Thus the distinctiveness of humans (the use of tools to make tools, the use of words about words, *RM* 178) will lead Burke to assert that words about words are also words about God. Such a conclusion is incipient in the description of Marx as a rhetorician of the sublime: 'The "theology" that Marx detected in "ideological mystification" is the *last reach of the persuasive principle itself*' (*RM* 179). Demystification must, if carried through, end with the mystical. There is a logic evident in Burke's having ended the 'Motivorum' project not with the promised volume 'On human relations' but with a *Rhetoric of Religion* in 1961. Rhetoric and theology are alike concerned with restitution, or with atonement: 'Empirically, what theologians discuss as the ultimate Oneness of God is equivalent to the ultimate oneness of the linguistic principle. Rhetoric is thus made from fragments of dialectic' (*RM* 175–6). This is an argument which proceeds by analogy, but the 'ground' to which Burke continually returns for all analogy is a theological one. In 'Definition of Man' he discusses the implications of Freud's 'displacement' as a rhetorical trope:

> Substitution sets the conditions for 'transcendence', since there is a technical sense in which the name for a thing can be said to 'transcend' the thing named (by making a kind of 'ascent' from the realm of motion and matter to the realm of essence and spirit). The subterfuges of euphemism can carry this process still further, culminating in the resources of idealization that Plato perfected through his dialectic of the Upward Way and Downward Way.
>
> (*LSA* 8–9)

This is a grosser (de-idealized) reiteration of the ending of *A Rhetoric of Motives* (1950). This ending is a Shelleyan speculation on hierarchy and the ascent of hierarchy, or transcendence: a 'range of mountings' culminating in a 'total mounting' towards order or identity (*RM* 313), in which symbolic instances are fragments of such a totality:

> Mysticism is no rare thing. True, the attaining of it in its pure state is rare. And its secular analogues, in grand or gracious symbolism, are rare. But the need for it, the itch, is everywhere. And by hierarchy it is intensified.
>
> (*RM* 332)

The 'mountings' of a hierarchy, whether sexual, Aristotelian or Christian are all functionally similar: 'the strivings of an entire series head in God as the beloved cynosure and sinecure, the end of all desire' (*RM* 333).

God is the terminus of rhetoric. All hierarchy entails an ordering principle which will function as both first and final term of a series: 'a body of positive terms must be brought to a head in a titular term which represents the principle or idea behind the positive terminology as a whole' (*RM* 189). Applied to Burke's own writings, this might well describe a trajectory which culminates in mysticism. The affirmations of the earlier work seem to await the God of negative theology: 'There is no "no" in music – and educators of children have also suggested the possibility that there is no "no" in the psychology of attention. The full strategy for saying "*don't* do that" is "*do* do this" ' (*ATH* 22). That observation, published in 1937, is more affirmative, more socially hopeful than Burke will become. Increasingly such hopefulness takes the form of a utopian (or mystic) desire for activity by which dialectic might not just be reversed (every no a yes) but cancelled. The revised edition of *Permanence and Change*, published in 1954, omits the pages in which the desired 'material co-operation' is named as communism but retains, at the end of Part II, this attempt to escape historical relativism by 'replacing the metaphor of progress ... with the metaphor of a *norm*':

> A sound system of communication, such as lies at the roots of civilization, cannot be built upon a structure of

economic warfare. The discordant 'sub-personalities' of the world's conflicting cultures and heterogeneous kinds of effort can be reintegrated only by means of a unifying 'master-purpose', with the logic of classification that would follow from it. The segregational, or dissociative state cannot endure – and must make way for an associative, or congregational state.

(PC 163)

Although Hegel is one of the thinkers consigned to the dustbin of historicism this looks like a Hegelian ideal. The desire is still current in the suggestions in *A Rhetoric of Motives* that rhetoric might lead us beyond rhetoric; that a ' "sociology of knowledge" ' or 'a "science" of social relations' will lead us to a new 'perfectly balanced vocabulary' of 'truth' and 'knowledge' (*RM* 199, 207).

So I am not arguing that Burke is a theologian *malgré lui*. As I hope to have shown here, four of his recurrent areas of concern – drama, grounds, history and rhetoric itself – culminate in a theological vocabulary, but that vocabulary consists of terms which can be infinitely substituted by others. Substitution, we remember, sets the conditions for transcendence – that last noun derives from a verb and refers to action. The transcendent, on the other hand, 'the last reach of the persuasive principle itself', is not an escape from tautology and paradox but precisely its 'last reach'. That is, beyond the desire for an end of rhetoric in association and the necessary defeat of that desire by the 'unanswerable opponent' of contingent circumstances lies the equally unanswerable fact of a vocabulary for that desire which is born out of its defeat. This can account, I think, for the way that even in what I have called the most systematizing of his books, *A Grammar of Motives*, the status of the five terms whose ratios Burke has elaborated at such length is thrown into doubt by his appending an essay on the 'master-tropes' of metaphor, metonymy, synecdoche and irony, which makes no reference to the preceding schema. This is not a confusion but accords with Burke's claims for symbolic action, which his own writings exemplify rather than merely comment on. Categorization and definition themselves depend on substitution and negation. So Burke's 'Dramatism' defines itself in opposition to definitions:

54

The 'scientistic' approach builds the edifice of language with primary stress upon a proposition such as 'It *is*, or it is not'. The 'dramatistic' approach puts the primary stress upon such hortatory expressions as 'thou *shalt*, or thou *shalt* not'.... Even if any given terminology is a *reflection* of reality, by its very nature as a terminology it must be a *selection* of reality; and to this extent it must function also as a *deflection* of reality.

(*LSA* 44–5)

The last sentence here is not only typical of Burke's manner but typical also in the way it assumes ultimate limits even as it crosses limits more immediately apparent.[4] This is the import of the 'mummery' of the electioneering fable at the end of 'The philosophy of literary form' and of positing an 'unanswerable opponent' in the same essay. 'Reality' in the quotation above is assumed, and is assumed to be distinct from both 'scientistic' and 'dramatistic' attempts at representing it. This suggests that there is a sphere in which occur both symbolic acts *and* descriptions after the event, propositions. There is also a separate sphere of events and actions which is impervious to attempts at representing it. This second sphere is called 'reality'.

Burke continues to acknowledge a duality of reality and a terminology for it, of action and symbolic action, and does acknowledge the secondariness of interpretation. Thus, strikingly, in 'War, response, and contradiction', an essay which Burke says 'literally terrified me at the time when I wrote it' (*DD* 20–1) in 1933, he prevents himself 'roaming into a region whereby even so contradictory an alignment as two armies opposed on a battlefield must seem like "cooperation" in the eyes of God' (*PLF* 251). There are limits, and these are not just the limits of language. There is an 'unanswerable opponent' recalcitrant to language yet language is the only possibility of answer; the resources of rhetoric are the only weapons of opposition. There are collective as well as natural events occurring outside of language yet language remains what we inhabit. Such events may occur outside language only in the sense that they are beyond the capabilities of interpretation. Through it we may nevertheless aspire to purify warfare. 'It's more complicated than that', as the Lord repeats at the end of *The Rhetoric of*

Religion. Swords are two-edged, and guns may be turned against their owners. In the next chapter I want first to consider Burke's notion of linguistic (or more generally symbolic) determinism and of its dangers; second to consider the way that this can for him be corrected or redeemed by comedy.

3

The spiritual counterpart of roadways

The last chapter traced the movement Burke discerns from conflict to community, the rhetorical ritual by which what is separate can be put together either by a sort of demonization – in the figure of the scapegoat – or by a more benign mystification, in the figure of the several names for the divine. The latter is a movement from conflict to communion. It takes rhetoric out of history and into a sphere of the essential. The temporal metaphor is seen to distort what rhetorical analysis discerns, partly because it substitutes the analysis for the actions analysed, and is therefore replaced by spatial metaphors. This chapter traces a similar movement in different terms. It investigates first the dangers, as Burke sees them, of commitment to any separate discourse, then, second, a recurrent trope of his own which relies on a spatial rather than a temporal metaphor and which, he claims, can overcome the blindness inherent to any such discourse by substituting a radically different point of view; finally it considers another kind of benign substitution by which conflicts can be translated and 'socialized' so that they come within the genre of comedy. If we are to take Burke seriously, or, as he says of the 'metaphor' of drama, *literally*, we have to see his writings participating in, and not merely describing such a movement.

This last claim is implied in something already instanced: near the end of the last chapter I quoted from the essay 'Terministic screens' in *Language as Symbolic Action* in which Burke distinguished two approaches to language. The 'scientist' approach is descriptive, or semantic: as he puts it elsewhere, its aim is '*to evolve a vocabulary that gives the name and address of every event*

57

in the universe' and thus it must ultimately be 'a fraud' (*PLF* 141, 159). In a lengthy discussion of Alfred Korzybski's *Science and Sanity* (see Korzybski 1948) in the section on 'Act' in the *Grammar of Motives* Burke deals with a sophisticated variant of the behaviourist, stimulus–response model he calls 'scientist'. Where 'scientism' is Platonic, nominalist, Dramatism is Aristotelian, realist; where the former requires a dictionary the latter requires a grammar:

> The realist Grammar ... begins with a *tribal* concept, and treats individuals as participants in this common substance, or element ... realism treats individuals as members of a group whereas nominalism treats groups as aggregates of individuals ... whereas realism treats generic terms as terms for *real* substances, nominalism treats them as merely conveniences of language.
>
> (*GM* 248)

Each approach however is caught within its own logic or consequential vocabulary, entailing some insight, some blindness – or, in Burke's terminology, 'choices between the principle of continuity and the principle of discontinuity' (*LSA* 50). The formula of 'terministic screens' names an insight on which Burke had long depended and which is expressed aphoristically in 'The philosophy of literary form': 'All questions are leading questions.... Every question selects a field of battle, and in this selection it forms the nature of the answers' (*PLF* 67). This is what he means by 'terministic screens': 'simply ... that any nomenclature necessarily directs the attention into some channels rather than others' (*LSA* 45). It is not that conclusions are implicit in premises argumentatively, rather that a given terminology can permit only certain conclusions while excluding others. Any terminology will aim towards an ultimate elaboration of its terms but only philosophy can hope for holistic description. In the 'comments' following the 'Terministic screens' essay Burke makes this claim:

> No matter how limited any particular philosopher's definition of man may be ... if he speaks as a philosopher he necessarily speaks 'in terms of' the *whole* man. For his

statement is philosophically complete only insofar as it involves a concept of man in general. In contrast, a special-ized scientific nomenclature (no matter how comprehensive it may be) necessarily involves *fragmenta-tion*. For no special discipline could be special except insofar as it defined man in terms of its specialty.

(*LSA* 57)

Perhaps it's surprising that Burke should salute the queen of all the sciences in this way, but he means by 'philosophy' a kind of analysis which, first, deals with humans, and therefore with action and second, does so holistically: that is, by taking all action as its province, therefore working with a 'concept' (if not definition) of humanity. To do otherwise, to be committed to specialized 'terministic screens' is to invoke large dangers. Spe-cialized discourses will exclude considerations relevant to the good of the whole in favour of those relevant only to the 'fragmented' concept on which the discourse rests. When Burke settles on 'rotten with perfection' as the final clause of his own 'Definition of Man' (*LSA* 16) he is summarizing a danger ad-verted to throughout his work.

Burke calls the impulse towards revealing the ultimate im-plications of a chosen vocabulary 'going to the end of the line'. The phrase occurs in his description of the process of extrapola-tion from a particular set of imagery to its participation in a wider symbolic set: 'over-all terms ... make even the most concrete of imageries "symbolic" or "representative" of one class or another', and this can be called ' "going to the end of the line" ' (*PLF* 83). At the end of the line, as we saw, is God: that which exists without a context. But extremes meet, and at the end of the line too is God's opposite. This is the movement of 'socialization' culminating in a scapegoat – for example, Hitler on the Jew (*PLF* 191–220). Analytically, even this movement, requiring the corrections of subsequent differentiation, 'lead[s] us quickly back into ingredients of social texture operating in the situation behind the writer's strategy' (*PLF* 84), but the process operates independently of any analysis of it. In *Perma-nence and Change* Burke describes a motive of perfection or, in Aristotelian terms, an ' "entelechial" principle' which is the temptation to pursue the logic of a terminology to its ends (*PC*

292–4). Where temptation exists, somewhere it will not be re-
sisted, and it is not that philosophy has a sense of decorum
which is lacking in other disciplines. ('The business of philosophy automatically commits one to … search for the wholes from
which parts derive their meaning' (*PC* 230).) Rather, the ' "entelechial" principle' entails all discourses tending to their
ultimate ends; most will do so however by excluding terms not
essential to their specialism.

Rhetoric for Burke is 'concerned with the state of Babel after
the Fall' (*RM* 23), a state which is historicized later in *A Rhetoric
of Motives*:

> the extreme division of labour under late capitalist liberal-
> ism having made dispersion the norm and having
> transformed the state of Babel into an ideal, the true liberal
> must view almost as an affront the Rhetorical concern with
> identification whereby the principles of a specialty cannot
> be taken at their face value, simply as the motives proper
> to that specialty. They *are* motives proper to the specialty
> *as such*, but not to the specialty as *participant in a wider
> context of motives*.
>
> (*RM* 30–1)

For the analyst (a 'true liberal'), one reaction to this situation is
to refuse the imperative of 'going to the end of the line', and this
tends to be Burke's reaction in the earlier books – 'We advocate
nothing, then, but a return to inconclusiveness' (*CS* 91). Of
course this depends on 'our' absolute freedom. We are not
enrolled in institutions or committed to vocabularies whose
terms (and thus whose ends) are not ours. The very logic implicit
in their terms – for Burke, a 'terministic compulsion' – means
that specialist discourses are always dangerous:

> Each such specialty is like the situation of an author who
> has an idea for a novel, and who will never rest until he has
> completely embodied it in a book. Insofar as any of these
> terminologies happen also to contain the risks of destroying
> the world, that's just too bad; but the fact remains that, so
> far as the sheer principles of the investigation are con-
> cerned, they are no different from those of the writer who

strives to complete his novel. There is a kind of 'terministic compulsion' to carry out the implications of one's terminology, quite as if an astronomer discovered by his observations and computations that a certain wandering body was likely to hit the earth and destroy us, he would nonetheless feel compelled to *argue for the correctness of his computations*, despite the ominousness of the outcome.

(*LSA* 19)[1]

Even such a notion of compulsion has a hopeful slant. To see such tasks as 'perfecting new powers of chemical, bacteriological or atomic destruction' (*RM* 30) as essentially versions of the writer's task is to presume them susceptible to the same kinds of analysis. In part this is evidently a Romantic inheritance, out of Nietzsche – as when Burke remarks in *Permanence and Change* that 'all life has been likened to the writing of a poem, though some people write their poems on paper, and others carve theirs out of jugular veins' (*PC* 76). On the other hand, symbolic action *is* distinct from action. The Romantic legacy is from Kant as well as from Nietzsche. The early insistence on the autonomy (and the ineffectuality) of the aesthetic is maintained. As J. L. Austin is drawn to a criterion of appropriateness ('happiness' or 'felicity') rather than 'truth' or success for judging the efficacy of the speech-act so Burke wants a similar criterion for judging the symbolic act:

> The ideal word is in itself an act, its value contained in its use at the moment of utterance. Its worth does not reside in its 'usefulness' and promise (though that is certainly a part of it) but in its *style* as words, as petition, in the *quality* of the petition, not in the *success* of the petition. For preparations, anything may serve, everything does serve – but preparations must not usurp the guise of fulfillments.
>
> (*PLF* 167)

Other discourses have other ends, but they can still be interpreted through terms drawn from the analysis of literary forms. Burke will come to call the 'screens' or 'compulsion' implicit in a discourse a principle of entelechy. He will define human beings in part as being 'rotten with perfection' (*LSA* 16) and seek

61

to explain phenomena like pollution in terms of an ' "entelech-ial" principle'. So, at the end of *Dramatism and Development* Burke explains his satire 'Helhaven' as in part a demonstration of entelechy:

> On one of the all-night radio programs with which I some-times while away insomniac hours, I heard an ardent proponent of Technologism ... ridiculing reactionary ide-alists who kept asking whether it might be possible to clear up the pollution in Lake Erie. They should look forward, not back, he said – and rather than trying to clean up Lake Erie, they should pollute it ten times as much, then find a way to extract from its wastes a new kind of energy.
>
> (*DD* 54)

Earlier, a terminology drawn from literature and applied to action is more exuberantly used. It is rarely clear whether action or the symbolic action of literary forms has the priority. This for example is from *Attitudes Toward History*: 'Whatever "free play" there may be in esthetic enterprise, it is held down by the gravitational pull of historical necessities; the poetic forms are symbolic structures designed to equip us for confronting given historical or personal situations' (*ATH* 57). The apparent deter-minism of this statement is qualified by its context within a discussion of the limits of knowledge or action. Burke calls these 'frames of acceptance or of rejection' – terms which imply voli-tion as well as merely reaction. There is a good summary by Joseph R. Gusfield:

> Frames of acceptance are ... not forms of passivity but the terms of relationship. [Burke] uses two seminal thinkers as examples. Both Aquinas and Marx saw the existence of classes. For Aquinas they were punishment for the fall of man; for Marx a consequence of capitalist exploitation. Aquinas' program was one of passive acceptance; Marx's a program for revolution. Both are forms of order and hierarchy, for in each there is a higher and a lower state of being. Each forms a mode of understanding and explana-tion. Aquinas justifies the order of class. Marx attacks it.
>
> (Gusfield 1989b: 47)

The 'poetic categories' Burke elaborates are categories of adjustment or adaptation to the *status quo*. Thus epic, tragedy and
comedy all tend towards its acceptance, and to be positive, while
elegy, satire and burlesque all tend towards its rejection, and to
be negative. There and elsewhere Burke associates his work with
comedy, but he also finds he needs a third category containing
the grotesque and the mystical (represented for example by
Blake) which deals with *re*adjustment, with incongruity. These
functions characterize much of Burke's writing and suggest one
of his better known terms.

Part II of *Permanence and Change* is entitled 'Perspective by
incongruity', a term which summarizes a variety of examples of
argument by analogy. It is indeed an argument *for* argument by
analogy to which we will return. Burke uses the term heavily in
Attitudes Toward History before defining it in that book's 'Dictionary of pivotal terms'. The entry for 'Perspective by incongruity'
defines it as a method counter to the authority of 'custom': 'A
method for gauging situations by verbal "atom cracking". That
is, a word belongs by custom to a certain category – and by
rational planning you wrench it loose and metaphorically apply
it to a different category' (*ATH* 308). It is a linking on a rational
basis of what is disparate, as a pun links words on a phonic basis.
An earlier entry, on 'Bureaucratization of the imaginative', contains a reference to the retention in science (which is the
'bureaucratization of Wisdom') of some unquestioned process
grounded only in 'the authority of custom':

> Our formula, 'perspective by incongruity', is a parallel
> 'methodology of invention' in the purely conceptual
> sphere. It 'bureaucratizes' the 'mass production' of per-
> spectives. It 'democratizes' a resource once confined to a
> choice few of our most 'royal' thinkers. *It makes perspectives
> cheap and easy.*
>
> (*ATH* 228–9)

Thus the concept has a Blakean ambition 'to "remoralize" by
accurately naming a situation already demoralized by
inaccuracy' – Blake rather than, say, Wilde, Burke would claim,
because of the heuristic or communally available quality of the
method. ' "Perspectives by incongruity" do not belong to a cult

of virtuosity, but bring us nearest to the simple truth' (*ATH* 309). Truth, as someone said, is rarely pure and never simple, but Burke claims that the method allows for active (if not antagonistic) participation in discourse: 'In sum, we contend that "perspective by incongruity" makes for a *dramatic* vocabulary, with weighting and counter-weighting, in contrast with the liberal ideal of *neutral* naming in the characterization of processes' (*ATH* 311). We shall need to return to that distinction of action from antagonism within discourse, for the insistence on partiality here (even from the metaphor of a *perspective*) certainly entails conflict. A much later (1972) summary suggests its usefulness as a means of seeing beyond our 'terministic screens' – or at least of rearranging the screens:

> Basically, the concept of 'perspective by incongruity' embodies the assumption that certain clusters of terms spontaneously exclude certain other clusters of terms; and these clusters tend to be kept apart, as though in different bins, unless a thinker who is in some respect 'perverse' suddenly bridges the gap…. If … spontaneous, mutually exclusive groupings are a kind of 'piety', then a 'planned incongruity' that violated such uncriticized assumptions would be a kind of 'impiety' that produced a new perspective by joining the 'naturally' disjunct. It would jolt our expectations.
>
> (*DD* 18)

If there is a claim for a kind of heroism there, flouting what a given period holds as custom or as piety, the method is also symptomatic – a reflex of such determinism. So in the later prologue to *Permanence and Change* Burke says that 'perspective by incongruity' is just another term for 'division' (*PC* xiii). 'A way of seeing is also a way of not seeing' (*PC* 49) and the new or ironic perspective holds no privileges over that to which it responds. Hence Burke's need to locate a perspective of perspectives at the end of *Grammar of Motives* (503–19) and in *The Rhetoric of Religion*, but the unease is present even in the elucidation of the term in the 'Dictionary of pivotal terms' in *Attitudes Toward History*, where it is held out against relativism, for integration, synthesis:

at one period ... artists were attempting to introduce a variety of perspectives, seeing the same objects from many sides at once. And after they had made such purely disintegrative attempts at analysis for a time, they began to search for a master perspective that would establish a new unity atop the shifts. Was not this concern akin to Einstein's method, whereby he gets shifting frames of reference, but co-ordinates their relativity with reference to the speed of light as a constant?

(ATH 310)

As the example shows, the period referred to is the 'modern'. Just as perspective depends on an individual – stressing her 'point of view' – the reduction or disintegration suggested here is consistent with the end of the individual. In *Permanence and Change* Burke had characterized the nineteenth century as 'transitional, or romantic in the extreme.... In the main, the Occidental world was approaching the *terminus ad quem* implicit in the individualistic movement formally inaugurated with the Renaissance' (*PC* 169). Burke here finds in the modern what Schiller's 'naïve' and 'sentimental' dichotomy found in Romanticism. To come of age is to find oneself belated; coming to consciousness is coming to a disabling self-consciousness. Identity and division can themselves be identified. It is an identification which can be made only from a viewing position which is at once both inside and outside what is viewed. Viewing, implicit to a metaphor of perspective, remains literal rather than metaphoric. Another pictorial example offered in the 'Dictionary' is in the caricatures of George Grosz, a surrealism which results in 'a perspective with interpretative ingredients' (*ATH* 311).

Surrealism is a good example of perspective by incongruity, a term which *Permanence and Change* clarifies by reference to Nietzsche and to Spengler – Burke reviewed and translated portions of *The Decline of the West* in the 1920s and devotes some pages to it in *Counter-Statement* – but which is implicit in the 'aesthetic' reading of Gourmont in *Counter-Statement.* Perspective by incongruity may be the vigour of a decadent, or a dying culture:

The crumbling and conflict of values certainly puts new burdens upon the artist – but on the other hand, it facilitates certain kinds of artistic endeavor which, in a stabilized structure, might be possible to the wayward individual but would not be very highly rated by his group.... Grotesque inventions flourish *when it is easiest to imagine the grotesque,* or *when it is hardest to imagine the classical....* One sees perspectives beyond the structure of a given vocabulary when that structure is no longer firm.

(PC 117)

Perspective is used in the sense in which it is used in the visual arts but the socialization of a perspective is not in the power of the individual artist. There is a kind of *Zeitgeist,* a discourse which can naturalize the individual's acts of denaturalization. Perspective by incongruity, and its socialization, cuts both ways. Neither the perception of 'division' nor the response to it is unitary. Perspective by incongruity can have a dissociative or more sinister function 'as when rulers silence domestic controversy by turning public attention to animosity against some foreign country's policies ... in this way ... antithesis helps reinforce unification by scapegoat' (*LSA* 19). Burke's own vocabulary in *Permanence and Change* is full of words like action, participation, co-operation, communication – the nineteenth century, he says, had stressed conflict over communication. For Burke as for Schiller the modern is to be characterized principally by its self-consciousness, but this is not the self-consciousness of an individual but of a culture at a particular stage:

Meaning or symbolism becomes a central concern precisely at that stage when a given system of meanings is falling into decay. In periods of firmly established meanings, one does not *study* them, one *uses* them: One frames his acts in accordance with them.

(PC 162)

Discourses are symptomatic, are responsive or functional. In his first book, *Counter-Statement,* Burke is visibly shifting from an account of this response as one personal to the writer to an account in which it is seen as indicative of the concerns of a social group at a particular period in their history – 'the shift from "self-expression" to "communication" ' (*LSA* 305). By the time of *Permanence and Change* – the Depression – such an account is integral to Burke's thinking. As the passage just quoted continues: 'in the last analysis, men do not communicate by a neutral vocabulary. In the profoundest human sense, one communicates by a *weighted* vocabulary in which the weightings are shared by his group as a whole' (*PC* 162). This contention will allow Burke a perspective in which oppositions can be overcome by calling attention to the way they inhabit the same discursive 'frame' or 'terministic screen'. The essay 'Semantic and poetic meaning' begins by noting the way differences become transformed into oppositions by slighting or overlooking the 'margin of overlap' between them (*PLF* 138–9). The reconciliatory function of the interpreter equates her with the 'curative' function of the text she considers. The function is a similar one whether its end is 'co-operation', to 'purify warfare' or to draw out the absurd but logical 'ends' of a particular terminology. These three alternatives correlate roughly with the early, middle and late phases of Burke's writing career, but the function can be seen clearly in *A Rhetoric of Motives* where he argues for 'identification' as the principle of rhetoric:

> In sum: Either elegant or filthy language can represent the hierarchic principle, just as both 'up' or 'down' represent the 'principle of height'…. In this way extremes can meet. To call a man very moral or to call him very immoral is at least 'the same' in the sense that, in both cases, one is saying, 'This man is to be considered exceptional from the standpoint of moral considerations' – and that is one of the purely 'grammatical' factors behind 'ambivalence' that might otherwise seem merely 'irrational'.
>
> (*RM* 258)

Hierarchies run in both directions, but it is difficult to find a vantage point from within a hierarchy in which this is visible. The articulations of a particular grammar will be disguised by what seems to be competition and dissociation. It is only from a vantage point outside that a congregationalist or co-operative impulse can be identified. Methodologically, a process which

67

would reverse the common translation of differences into oppositions and would show how apparently opposed positions
employ the same grammar or terminology, must end in tautology – or in God. Near the beginning of his 'Curve of history' in
Attitudes Toward History the spiritual possibilities of such a
two-way street have their 'counterpart' rather in imperialism:
'A roadway constructed by a power expanding westward could
be retrod by a western power expanding eastward. The same
applies to the habits of thought that are the spiritual counterpart
of roadways' (*ATH* 112). In *A Rhetoric of Motives* Burke defends
his position with a significantly different analogy:

> We are not merely trying to strike a compromise between
> unreconcilable opponents, or treating the two positions as
> ideal opposites, with the truth somewhere in between.
> Rather, we are assigning a definite function to each of the
> positions – and we are saying that, insofar as each performs
> its function, they are no more at odds than the stomach and
> liver of a healthy organism.
>
> (*RM* 137)

In *The Rhetoric of Religion* Burke insists that his concern is with
words about God rather than with God; and though he has
remained fascinated by but shy of theology more and more he
has written what is, in effect, anthropology. The use of words,
the deployment of symbols, is the definitively human activity.
The corporeal analogy just quoted will aspire to be a literal
description rather than an analogy. As this quotation suggests,
even the Burke of his middle period will explain and defend his
methodology in terms of its holistic possibilities. Irony may
become tautology; the end of incongruity is congruity. Burke
does privilege his method with an Olympian perspective and
does imply a potential for cure as well as merely for diagnosis.
This accounts, I think, for his dislike of a phenomenon apparently similar to 'perspective by incongruity' – what he calls
'debunking' or 'muckraking'.

In an essay on 'The virtues and limitations of debunking'
published in 1938 and reprinted in *The Philosophy of Literary Form*
Burke defines it thus:

It refers in general to that class of literature designed to show that George Washington did not cut down the cherry tree, and the highly alembicated versions of such. It counters the inflating of reputations by the deflating of reputations. It is the systematic 'let down' that matches the systematic 'build up'. At one time in America an aspect of it went by the name of 'muckraking'.

(*PLF* 168)

In *Permanence and Change* it is said that the technique cannot go far enough. It would identify a Bad Guy (a kind of radical scapegoat) and would assume that once the aberrant individual is replaced society would be purged:

The period of muckraking in American journalism was largely wasted because the writers so often assumed that certain 'wicked' people were doing the damage to our society, and that if only 'good' people were put in their stead, all would be well. But the trouble did not arise so much from abnormal greed, as from defects in our social and political organization whereby the effects of normal greed are so amplified that they have the effects of abnormal greed.

(*PC* 204)

Burke will come to efface the commonsensical distinction made here between 'defective' or 'abnormal' and 'normal' social tendencies. In the later piece debunking is traced to Hobbes and Machiavelli, to sceptical versions of society which begin not from the virtues but from the vices:

Machiavelli tended to consider the 'ungrateful, deceitful, cowardly, and greedy' aspects of men not as an aspect of their 'fall', but as the very *essence* of their nature. Lying was not a *deviation* from the norm, it *was* the norm.

(*PLF* 169).

In the chapter on 'Comic correctives' in *Attitudes Toward History* Burke traces a more recent line, from Bentham (whose paternity in debunking is also stressed in the 1938 essay), and shows a moral distaste for its reductiveness:

For though the doctrine of *Zweck im Recht* is a veritable Occam's razor for the simplification of human motives, teaching us the role that *special material interests* play in the 'impartial' manipulations of the law, showing us that law can be privately owned like any other property, it can be too thorough; in lowering human dignity so greatly, it lowers us all.

(*ATH* 166)

What Burke moves to then is his own kind of 'identification' by which he claims that vice and virtue, normal and abnormal, upwards and downwards, exposition and exhortation can be reconciled, and encompassed within the fuller perspective of what he will come to call Dramatism.

Later in 'The virtues and limitations of debunking' essay Burke nails his colours to the mast:

I see no good reason, except perversities arising in response to the complexities of our times, why one should have to treat the *exposition* of human motives as synonymous with the *debunking* of human motives. And I hold that, if one refuses to accept this equation, one may seek rather such perspectives as interpret human events by making scientific diagnosis and moral exhortation integral aspects of one program.

(*PLF* 189)

The disintegrations of perspective by incongruity require a re-integration; at a more abstract level than this, Bentham (or Nietzsche, or Hegel) can be countered with another of Burke's recurrent sources, Bergson:

Instead of looking for an Hegelian synthesis that would follow thesis and antithesis, he would have us realize that the real course of events is necessarily, at all times, unified.... In cases where the synthetic word does not happen to be already given, he suggests we should get it by combining the antithetical ones.

(*PC* 94)

The movement from 'conflict' to 'communication' is always a movement that goes back beyond the acknowledgement of competing interests. It is a movement that goes back beyond the 'historicism' of the nineteenth century to a prehistoric or timeless and essential foundation. The discomfiting *comfort* of perspective by incongruity – or of debunking, or muckraking – requires that it be set against a synthesizing or essentializing role for the interpreter:

> Can one, writing today and reviewing this accrued indi-
> vidualism of prophetic insight, feel that there is anything
> to be done but find his own point of view and add it to the
> general medley? Or may he ask himself whether the theo-
> ries of 'truth' really are as manifold as such a picture of our
> modern Babel would lead him to suspect? And instead of
> noting the great variety of religious, metaphysical, ethical,
> and psychological lore, might we try rather to detect the
> strains which run through it all? Might we take the varia-
> tions not as essential, but as contingent?
>
> (*PC* 181)

This is an argument for essentialism, for invariant factors (or even 'truths') which it behoves the interpreter to acknowledge. Burke wrote of the literary text in the 1930s 'first genus, then differentia'. I have argued that this can lead to the appeasement of the social as well as the literary text. Others have tried to enlist Burke for a harmless relativism.[2]

Burke himself ends the 'Terministic screens' essay from *Language as Symbolic Action* with a pre-emptive defence against the charge of 'mere relativism'. He claims at this point that his 'Dramatism' does not require a grounding in anthropological, biological (or, presumably, metaphysical) definition – though he can still gesture at a notion of ' "collective revelation" ' some-where in prehistory. This emerges as a 'tribal speech' which assumes a distinction between things and persons in intuiting a distinction between motion and action by which they are respec-tively defined. There is a *reductio ad absurdum* of this argument – 'even the behaviorist who studies man in terms of his laboratory experiments, must treat his colleagues as *persons*, rather than purely and simply as automata responding to stimuli' (*LSA* 53)

– but Burke's claim here is that the grounding definition does not have to be made; it is enough that we behave as though it had been made, without having to make it. His project is thus interpretative, superstructural and hopeful:

> whether or not we are just things in motion, we think of one another ... as *persons*.... For the sake of the argument, I'm even willing to grant that the distinction between *things moving* and *persons acting* is but an illusion. All I would claim is that, illusion or not, the human race cannot possibly get along with itself on the basis of any other intuition.
>
> (*LSA* 53)

This is hopeful, and hopeful in its pragmatism rather than despite its pragmatism. It's an instance in which we recognize a tension between the pragmatist (or Emersonian) Burke and the system-building (or Blakean) Burke. His Dramatism does ultimately depend upon such unprovable intuitions – 'Dramatism would feel safest if one could prove beyond all doubt (as one doubtless never will) that everything in the realm of physics and biology is inexorably determined' (*DD* 81). Taking the pragmatist route however would mean Burke having to forgo the possibility of prophecy or speculation in favour of retrospective analysis. 'Definition' is almost always retrospective, as we have seen, and from the fifties Burke practises the retrospective derivation of complex systems from the givens of their vocabularies, calling this 'prophecy after the event'.

Burke would argue that teleology has been given a bad name. And the *telos* within which he has wanted to situate his own work has been comedy, the form which would subsume division under identification. The *Grammar of Motives*, Burke says,

> began with a theory of comedy, applied to a treatise on human relations. Feeling that competitive ambition is a drastically over-developed motive in the modern world, we thought this motive might be transcended if men devoted themselves not so much to 'excoriating' it as to 'appreciating' it.
>
> (*GM* xvii).

I have dwelt on some of Burke's recurrent terms in, principally, his work of the thirties, because the instability of the terms – an instability upon which he gleefully insists – is claimed to be what is merely adequate for representing the instability of the historical period in which they are identified and used. 'Perspective by incongruity' is both an action and a reaction; both a technique for dividing up arguments in new ways and a name for divisions which are perceived to exist. Burke rejects the possibility of the technique being idiosyncratic, possible only to the 'virtuoso' interpreter and thereby retains in it this crucial ambiguity. If history is not to be seen as determinate and determining, then it must be seen to act according to principles which should also be the principles by which it is interpreted. So Burke's critique of 'debunking' and 'muckraking' is founded primarily on a moral 'intuition' – the intuition that fundamental motives need not be base motives. He wants then to find in history not only aesthetics but also ethics. It could be argued of course that these concerns are only a preparation for theoretical work which will simply omit the messiness of contingency, leaving an aesthetics and an ethics drained of the history to which they are an answer – and to which, we might want to argue, they must answer – but this is not quite my argument. Burke wants a kind of interpretation that can be prospective or predictive and not only responsive. The two published 'Motives' books group their examples under headings which are more obviously stages of a linear argument than in *Permanence and Change* or *Attitudes Toward History*, and the *Grammar* in particular has ambitions that cannot themselves be contained for inclusiveness. It can seem to want to include the contingent possibilities from which conclusions may be drawn, as well as the local arguments that lead to these conclusions, and the conclusions themselves. Calling this a quixotic ambition is only to call these writings ultimately comic in genre and not only *about* the genre of comedy.

The co-operative or integrational impulses of the *Grammar* are continued from *Attitudes Toward History* where what is merely desired blurs into what is described: the conclusion to Part I of that book hopes

to have so weighted our discussion that the comic frame will appear the most serviceable for the handling of human

73

relationships. It avoids the dangers of euphemism that go with the more heroic frames of epic and tragedy. And thereby it avoids the antithetical dangers of cynical debunking, that paralyze social relationships by discovering too constantly the purely materialistic ingredients in human effort.

(*ATH* 107)

Later in the same book comedy is claimed to be a synthesis, correcting the overemphases to which antithesis itself is prone: so the antithetical descriptions of man as a citizen of heaven and man as a jungle-dweller would be 'transcended' by a description of man as *'man in society'*: 'as such it would come close to restoring the emphasis of Aristotle, with his view of man as a "political animal" ' (*ATH* 169–70). Comedy comes between the antitheses of 'euphemism' and 'debunking'. There is, Burke writes later, transcendence downwards as well as upwards. Transcendence upwards takes the linguistic form of euphemism, the motive 'done for God', transcendence downwards is associated with debunking, with materialist explanations of motive, 'done purely for gravy' (*ATH* 336–8):

In the motives we assign to the actions of ourselves and our neighbors, there is implicit a program of socialization.... A comic frame of motives ... would not only avoid the sentimental denial of materialistic factors in human acts. It would also avoid the cynical brutality that comes when such sensitivity is outraged, as it must be outraged by the acts of others or by the needs that practical exigencies place upon us.

The comic frame, in making man the student of himself, makes it possible for him to 'transcend' occasions when he has been tricked or cheated, since he can readily put such discouragements in his 'assets' column, under the head of 'experience'. Thus we 'win' by subtly changing the rules of the game – and by a mere trick of bookkeeping, like the accountants for big utility corporations, we make 'assets' out of 'liabilities'.

(*ATH* 170–1)

The translation involved here is partly that colloquial (or folksy) sense of 'being philosophical' about things ('heads I win, tails you lose' (*ATH* 260–3)); its consolatory purpose is the purpose of religion too (as atonement). Such 'comic' accommodation offers the intellectual an alternative, more socially efficacious than 'moral indignation'; it offers 'abatement' but not 'recompense' of alienation:

> The comic frame of acceptance but carries to completion the translative act. It considers human life as a project in 'composition', where the poet works with the materials of social relationships. Composition, translation, also 'revision', hence offering maximum opportunities for the resources of *criticism*.
>
> (*ATH* 173)

Comedy then figures as a translation, of which there are paradigms in the proverbial or advisory translations of literary works or of proverbs themselves as we saw them described in the 'Literature as equipment for living' essay. At the end of the second section of that essay Burke talks, as he does here, of a ' "folk criticism" ' on the analogy of 'folk art'. In this earlier essay Burke describes such terms as

> a collective philosophy of motivation, arising to name the relationships, or social situations, which people have found so pivotal and so constantly recurring as to need names for them. The metaphorical migration of a term from some restricted field of action into the naming of acts in other fields is a kind of 'perspective by incongruity' that we merely propose to make more 'efficient' by proposing a *methodology* for encouraging still further metaphorical migrations.
>
> (*ATH* 173)

Such linguistic 'migrations' are not contingent or opportunistic but constitute 'a collective philosophy of motivation' already in colloquial existence. In his work of the thirties, and through the 'Motivorum' project, Burke claims to provide this unmethodical 'philosophy' with its methodology. The collective sphere is not named, though it is clearly opposed to the various 'specialisms' which may partly constitute it. Nor is it to be associated with the movements of a hypostatized 'History': Burke comes to see division of labour for example as an anthropological rather than a historical phenomenon. This collective sphere is to be found instead in 'the people', the term Burke suggested be substituted for the term 'worker' at the American Writers' Congress in April 1935. (Burke's speech there, and the angry response to it, furnishes Lentricchia's book with its 'representative anecdote'.) This is a sphere which is taken not only to 'identify' class antagonisms but also to be transhistorical. This 'socialization' would cast the interpreter as a figure who, in effect, only transcribes a 'folk' philosophy, as the figure who represents a corporate author. Indeed it raises the problem of representation in the electoral as well as the rhetorical sense of that word. For now though it is enough to note that such socialization is a kind of secular atonement, an accommodation of circumstance to an essential desire. It is the frame of comedy which best explains the phenomenon of a recurrent metaphor:

> the metaphor of a *norm*, the notion that at bottom the aims and genius of man have remained fundamentally the same, that temporal events may cause him to stray far from his sources, but that he repeatedly struggles to restore, under new particularities, the same basic pattern of the 'good life'.
>
> (*PC* 163)

4

This alchemic centre

The claim that there is a 'norm' evident in contingent action is an essentializing claim. It assumes that there is a reality underlying the properties and functions of action and that these must therefore be merely appearances which are secondary and which derive from this reality. 'Comedy', 'acceptance' and 'rejection' (to use only some terms from the last chapter) are supra-historical 'frames', of which particular actions and sets of actions are only examples. While some of Burke's procedures are 'essentializing' in the way I have just described it, it should also be clear that much of his work involves an investigation and critique of essentialism. Of course it remains possible that this work is actually a symptom of what it seeks to diagnose but its reflexiveness or self-consciousness at least makes this charge more complicated to make. In this chapter I shall consider Burke's response to one such charge, made in a review; and his treatment of another term for 'essence', 'constitution'; but I want to begin with what can be seen as a pre-emptive response.

In an essay in *The Philosophy of Literary Form*, Burke charges Freud with essentialism. He distinguishes 'between what I should call an essentializing mode of interpretation and a mode that stresses proportion of ingredients. The tendency in Freud is towards the first of these' (*PLF* 261). This distinction actually depends on a sleight of hand. The honorific 'mode that stresses proportion of ingredients' is not simply the binary opposite of an 'essentializing mode'. The distinction is roughly akin to Saussure's diachrony/synchrony distinction, but in Burke's version the first term of this pair is not – as it might be called in less interested terms – an interpretation of historical changes but an

'essentializing mode' to be lumped for dismissal with 'the genetic fallacy' and 'historicizing'. Burke recommends
encountering the synchrony of Freudian terms rather than the
diachrony of Freudian narrative: 'Freud's terminology is a dictionary, a lexicon for charting a vastly complex and hitherto
largely uncharted field. You can't refute a dictionary. The only
profitable answer to a dictionary is another one' (*PLF* 272). (It
might be argued of course that a dictionary – even an etymolog-
ical dictionary – is concerned precisely with 'essentializing'.)
Whatever the justice or otherwise of describing Freudian techniques in particular as 'essentializing', it seems that causal
interpretation in general must be 'essentializing' and reductive.
A Freudian diagnosis – for Burke, an ascription of 'motivation'
– isolates a single cause of neurosis. This reduction of the complex to the simple is, Burke says, 'a normal ideal of science'
(another example he gives is 'economic determinism'), and it
inevitably falsifies:

> Now, I don't see how you can possibly explain the complex
> in terms of the simple without having your very success
> used as a charge against you. When you get through, all
> that your opponent need say is: 'But you have explained
> the complex in terms of the simple – and the simple is
> precisely what the complex is not.'
>
> (*PLF* 262)

Burke's own practice acknowledges that there is a place for
reductiveness, though it is always vulnerable to this charge – a
charge which centres on what is seen as the confusion of logical
with temporal priority, and too swift a movement from the
contingent and empirical (the world of appearances) to a single
'idea' from the transcendental or essential realm. There is a
contradiction though. It arises from describing as
'essentializing' a mode of interpretation that is actually concerned with historical change and difference while preferring,
as a mode presumably free of this tendency, a mode to which it
is peculiarly susceptible. This is, I think, a contradiction too
fundamental simply to be deplored, just as it should not be
simply glossed over. Thus I want to pursue Burke's critique of
ideology through his own pursuit not of the ascription of

'motives' (a transitive term), but of the intransitively essentializing terms 'grounds' and 'substance'.

This chapter focuses principally on three texts: Burke's reply to a review of his *Attitudes Toward History*, a reply which is reprinted in *The Philosophy of Literary Form*; the first section of Part III of *A Grammar of Motives*; and finally a passage from the introduction to the same book. In the first of these the adjective 'ideological' does appear, though the functions of ideology are displaced into other terms – partly, I suggest, into the term 'attitude', which is suggested as a sixth term to be added to the pentad of the *Grammar*. Then I move on to what is apparently an empirical example of the way interpretation 'grounds' itself by considering Burke's treatment of the United States Constitution in the *Grammar*. I think this shows, first, that a split between empirical and speculative, or between the theory and the practice of interpretation, cannot be sustained, but second, that the 'act' of 'substance' considered in Chapter 1 need not be left in paradox, which is where we left it there. Examples turn into metaphors, and 'substance' itself is shown to be soluble, but Burke's transformations are not, I argue, transformations of 'culture' into 'nature', of materialism into idealism. Thus the third text, written in a highly abstract or theoretical (indeed a metaphysical) mode, is concerned with distinctions – things which analytically don't fit a model, or that we want to particularize, or for which we want to make exceptions that may put pressure on the model itself. I want to begin however with a text which, however it may look like merely a local skirmish, is crucial to the working-out of Burke's methodology and leads to the head-on engagement with essentialism Burke will call 'the dialectic of constitutions'.

Burke published his 'Twelve propositions on the relation between economics and psychology' in the second volume of the American Marxist quarterly *Science & Society* in Spring 1938. The article is, in part, a synthesis of *Attitudes Toward History* in reply to a review of the book in the previous number of *Science & Society* by Margaret Schlauch, who was one of that journal's editors. Michael Feehan has drawn attention to this being a crucially transitional document, making lucidly, directly and for the first time 'the claim that drama is not a metaphor for but rather a model of human relations' (Feehan 1979: 405). It's also crucial for Burke personally – I think there is a rueful self-portrait in his example of the way an 'individual is composed of many "corporate identities" ': 'one may be identified with a general body of thought "oppositional" in quality, while at the same time making various attempts to identify himself with some specific political faction' (*PLF* 307). If I am right, then not only can we recognize a personal poignancy but also we can save ourselves from simple-minded inferences along the lines that Burke, seeing Marxism won't do, erects Dramatism in its place. 'Twelve propositions' is crucial too in the way it continues to 'identify' Burke's procedures with those of orthodox Marxism as well as 'opposing' them.

Schlauch's is an acute and critical, though not unsympathetic brief review – and not, as Feehan says, 'vehemently negative' (405). She recognizes, for example, the 'promiscuous application' of the metaphor of a frame in *Attitudes Toward History*, and notices the way Burke behaves as though 'to accept' were an intransitive verb:

> acceptance and rejection appear, not as natural reactions to historical objects, but as mysterious separate forces which must be dealt with and properly appeased before a communistic society can be established ... there can ... be no more acceptance in the epic than in the elegy and no more rejection in communism struggling against capitalism than in capitalism itself. In other words, forms of thought are given a position of primary importance in Burke's scheme of history, despite other passages which seem to disclaim this idealist emphasis.
>
> (Schlauch 1969: 106–7)

Schlauch picks out some silly passages from *Attitudes Toward History* and objects to the imposition of a synchronic (psychoanalytic, or even phonetic) grid onto history, warning of a danger in Burke's method 'that sheer emphasis may make it appear that economic development is subordinate to or dependent upon the history of poetic forms' (Schlauch 1969: 109).

Burke is silent about some of Schlauch's charges but he is concerned at this point to admit psychological motives to an economic account of history. Thus he can defend his terms 'acceptance' and 'rejection' as the psychological (or, in a revealing shift, the spiritual) counterparts of the materialist factors that account for historical change and Freud can be enlisted alongside Marx as an ideologue. The basic means by which to 'unite' Marx and Freud, which is the ambition Burke sets himself in 'Twelve propositions', is the concept of 'symbols of authority'. By 'symbols of authority' Burke means ideology: to reject them results in 'alienation'; to accept them secures 'identity'. Burke answers Schlauch's charge of 'mystification' by accepting the term but claiming it to be a homeopathic necessity rather than a symptom: '8. Identity itself is a "mystification". Hence, resenting its many labyrinthine aspects, we tend to call even the study of it a "mystification" ' (PLF 308). The article suggests that what can be studied, in daily life as well as works of art, are the strategies people employ to ' "own" privilege vicariously' or symbolically (PLF 309) by adopting the 'style' or 'insignia' of a privileged class: this is the 'identification' which will be the central term of A Rhetoric of Motives.

Feehan under-rates the extent to which Burke is still seeking an accommodation with orthodox Marxism by restating that his new model is commensurate with a base–superstructure model. Art 'reflects' the relations of the base: 'Art works ... are like "meter readings". Here all the implicit social processes become explicit' (PLF 308). The notion of the poet as meter reader is also still continuous with the aestheticism of Counter-Statement, with the notion of the poet (rather than the poem) as tuning-fork or antenna of the culture.

The later propositions do shift from a Marxist to a 'Dramatistic' vocabulary, within which the workings of ideology are named as 'secular prayer'. The Marxist vocabulary is held to be inadequate because of the cumbersomeness of having to demonstrate a direct, reflective relationship between superstructural ' "strategies" ' and the economic base:

9. The analysis of the 'strategies' by which men respond to the factor of alienation and by which they attempt to repossess their world could not be conducted without tremendous wastage of time and energy, if a writer were required, at every point, to stop and demonstrate the specific bearing of his analysis upon such matters as food, jobs, etc.

(PLF 308)

Interpretation should take what it is given by the aesthetic object – should traffic in the superstructure rather than speculating in a causal or 'genetic' fashion. Burke instances Shakespeare in this regard:

> new methods of production gave rise to the change from feudal to bourgeois values.... This 'superstructural' material was the objective, social material he manipulated in eliciting his audience's response. Economic factors gave rise to the transition in values, but he dealt with the transition in values.
>
> (*PLF* 309)

'Values' here are, it is insisted, ideological values to be considered intrinsically rather than extrinsically. Such values, he goes on, are always to do with identification which, in turn, is a symbolic identification with property; but then comes the significant shift. History is to be understood in terms of such literary forms, rather than attempting to understand literary forms in terms of historical forces. As Feehan points out, what was only a suggestion in Attitudes Toward History here becomes a programmatic statement. This is from Attitudes Toward History:

> One way of approaching the structures of symbolism might be profitably tested by the examination of various literary categories, as each of the great poetic forms stresses its own peculiar way of building the mental equipment (meanings, attitudes, character) by which one handles the significant factors of his time.
>
> (*ATH* 34)

This becomes the eleventh of the 'Twelve propositions': '*Human relations should be analysed with respect to the leads discovered by a study of drama*' (*PLF* 310). 'Various literary categories' become 'drama' and 'might be profitably tested' becomes 'should be analysed' (Feehan 1979: 407).

Changes of identity are dramatic, 'politics above all is drama' (*PLF* 310), and the rabbits practically jump out of the hat:

Both Freud and Marx were 'impresarios'. Marx's concept of the 'classless stage following a maximum intensification of class conflict' is precisely in line with the Aristotelian recipe for the process of dramatic 'catharsis'. The shock value of Freudian analysis exemplified the same process in tiny 'closet dramas' of private life (the facing and burning-out of conflict). Forms like the lyric ... are analyzable as 'monodrama'.

(*PLF* 311)

I have been quoting from the version of 'Twelve propositions' subsequently published in *The Philosophy of Literary Form*, but the original *Science & Society* version of the article has a significantly different ending. In the version in *The Philosophy of Literary Form* Burke concludes with an exhortation which is consistent with the books of the thirties: an exhortation to a dialectic of permanence with change, to an essential common ground for the study of symbolic action, which 'should avoid the coaching of *unnecessary* factional dispute by considering modes of response applicable to *all* men and it could confine differences solely to those areas where differences *are* necessary' (*PLF* 313). In the *Science & Society* version of the article Burke responds to a telling charge from Schlauch. She quotes his desire – omitted from the second edition – to 'recover a world of nouns, going from a philosophy of *processes* to a philosophy of *categories*', and comments that her Marxist readership 'are not apt to share this nostalgia for a medieval world of stable nouns. They have presumably made themselves at home in a world of verbs and change' (Schlauch 1969: 108). Rather than rebut the charge of 'nostalgia' Burke responds by pointing out the oddity, for anyone who claims to be a dialectical thinker, of feeling 'at home' in process. The verbal nouns of 'acceptance' and 'rejection' themselves suggest a way of holding permanence and change, the essential and the contingent together dialectically. Burke suggests a synthesizing term, 'process-categories', 'strategies' which 'maintain something permanent through flux, while at the same time they must adapt themselves to the specific changes of material provided by flux' (TwPr 249). A basic notion of such an inquiry is 'attitudes'.

In the 1983 afterword to *Attitudes Toward History*, 'attitude' is defined as 'the point of *personal mediation* between the realms of nonsymbolic motion and symbolic action' (*ATH* 394). It seems then that 'attitude' is another term for ideology. Certainly, Burke's argument for the importance of the added term suggests that it names something central to Dramatism and which cannot be straightforwardly accommodated within a realm of literal acts:

> The realm of the incipient, or attitudinal, is the realm of 'symbolic action' par excellence.... Here is the area of thought wherein actual conflicts can be transcended with results sometimes fatal, sometimes felicitous. But the study of its manifestations will vow us, at every step, to the study of that 'attitudinal action' which we have called the dramatistic, but which might also be called the dialectical.
>
> (*GM* 243)

We shall need to return to the complementarity of dramatism and dialectic asserted here, but for the moment it is the assertion of 'attitude' as 'the realm of "symbolic action" par excellence' that needs to be considered.

For the Burke of the thirties, 'an attitude contains an implicit program of action' (*PLF* 143). Literature for example is 'an incipient form of action ... an implied code of conduct' (*CS* 185). Of course, a 'code of conduct' seems not to be the complement of 'action'. It seems rather to be a summarizing or interpretative term which may retrospectively explain how acts can be grouped together, or can be used to predict future acts. It seems then that 'attitude' must have an odd status as a rhetorical term. Classical rhetoric is codified mainly as the means of oratorical persuasion. That is to say, it codifies a practice which results in another practice. For example, Aristotle, in opposing the soph- ists in his *'Art' of Rhetoric*, wants to make rhetoric a study of the means of persuasion not confined to one particular art but finding the proofs integral to any or all of them. Rhetoric then need not principally be concerned with writing at all, certainly not with 'literary' writings, and may need modifying as a means of explaining the effect of such writings. (If not modified, it would make no distinction between 'literature' and 'lying'.) I take this focus because Burke takes literary texts (poems by Wordsworth and Shelley) to exemplify the production of 'attitude'. There are then two problems here: first, whether rhetoric is an appropriate instrument for considering utterances in which the effect of 'persuasion' is not immediately evident, in which action is deferred; and second, related to this, whether Burke's 'symbolic action' enjoys any special status within an account of language generally.

We have seen already that 'persuasion' for Burke extends ultimately to ineffable 'action': 'the principle of persuasion, as reduced to its most universal form, leads to the theologian's attempt to establish an *object* of such prayer; namely: God' (*RM* 179). It is notable that what I called an extension Burke calls a reduction, and that he later adds: 'what we mean by pure persuasion in the absolute sense exists nowhere' (*RM* 269). As to the second problem, Burke does find he needs to make distinctions, which involves making a hierarchy: 'Whereas poetic language is a kind of symbolic action, for itself and in itself, and whereas scientific action is a preparation for action, rhetorical language is inducement to action (or to attitude, attitude being an incipient act)' (*RM* 42). Burke complicates the definition of rhetoric not only by adding a definition of it as 'identification' but by adding to its traditional definition as persuasion the explanation that it can be persuasion to *attitude* rather than directly to action. He says in the foreword to *The Rhetoric of Religion* that religion is a fit subject for rhetoric because it aims to persuade by forming 'the kinds of attitude which prepare men for action'. Furthermore, the notion of attitude allows Burke to reintroduce a category of the poetic (primarily of the lyric poem) as a category of wholly intrinsic acts which do not result in their readers being persuaded to action:

> the notion of persuasion to *attitude* would permit the application of rhetorical terms to purely *poetic* structures; the study of lyrical devices might be classed under the head of rhetoric, when these devices are considered for their power to induce or communicate states of mind to readers, even though the kinds of assent evoked have no overt, practical outcome.
>
> (*RM* 50)

The chapter ' "Incipient" and "delayed" action' in the section on

'Act' in the *Grammar of Motives* musters I. A. Richards (who has a chapter on 'Attitude' in *The Principles of Literary Criticism*), G. H. Mead, Alfred Korzybski and Aristotle, together with examples from Wordsworth and Shelley, in support of the contention that an incipient act can be the introduction to or preparation for an act, or that it can substitute for an act: 'an attitude of sympathy may either lead to an act of sympathy, or it may serve as substitute for an act of sympathy' (*GM* 242). Later, Burke records his regret that he did not make the *Grammar's* pentad into a hexad by adding the term 'attitude'. As it stands, the term 'agency' covers two different orders of description. 'Agency' answers the question: 'how was an action performed?'; but that question may be answered 'with a hammer' or 'with gusto'. The second answer ought to be put under the heading of 'attitude'. Burke reflects that 'possibly purely personal motives may have affected my original choice of pentad rather than an explicit hexad' (*DD* 23) and in the *All-Area* interview he recalls a letter referring to his children as 'my five terms' (C-G 18; C 302-3). Cary Nelson comments on 'the sense that his categories are wilfully hypostatized and even personified, so that they become the dramatis personae of his intellectual family romance' (Nelson 1989: 164), and we would be right to be suspicious of a totalizing system which can so cheerfully admit its arbitrary foundations. Yet this also suggests that his increasing stress on 'attitude' as a supplement to the pentad will allow Burke to readmit the freely willing and choosing subject as the source and arbiter of all acts. The socially constructed 'identity' of 'Twelve propositions' is here extended by 'attitude' – anticipation of the 'attitudes' of the other helps to form the self (*GM* 237).

In 1978, in the summarizing essay '(Nonsymbolic) Motion/(Symbolic) Action', Burke returns to Richards' chapter on 'Attitudes' to draw a 'behavioristic parallel'. He adds to Richards' definition of 'attitude' as 'incipient or future action' the claim that it is always in the present because it always shows corporeally or physiologically: 'it must be by some means grounded in the set of the body now', and this grounding shows conjugations of a verb to be 'bodily conjugated' – the dog salivates ('I will eat'), eats, and curls up to go to sleep ('I have eaten') ((N)M/(S)A 816). Burke's argument with behaviourism (which for him is the type of all science) leads him provocatively to choose a Pavlovian example. 'Attitude' here is so extended as to designate any kind of response to a stimulus. This extended sense of 'attitude' loses much of the distinctiveness of the term – it can be response to symbols, or a wholly physiological response ((N)M/(S)A 815). Nevertheless it continues to stress that 'attitude' is the mediating function between motion and action: 'The mental *attitude* ... must have some corresponding bodily *posture'* (*GM* 242).

I have suggested that 'attitude' is a supplement accommodating a liberal humanist subject which cannot itself be reaccommodated to the interpretative transformations of the *Grammar's* terms. In the chapter from the *Grammar*, 'attitude' also introduces a concept of the symbolic act as intrinsic, autonomous and self-contained – a concept which cannot really be distinguished from a New Critical concept of the poem. The preparatory and substitutive senses of 'attitude' can be displaced into the 'dramatic' and the 'lyrical'. Of course it is drama which has the priority, even when considering the lyric poem as a form. Where 'Twelve propositions' calls lyric 'monodrama' (*PLF* 311), the *Grammar's* chapter calls the form the realm of 'attitudes':

> *images* can have the force of attitudes. Hence, when analyzing the structure of a lyric (a form in which there is no act in the full dramatic sense) we may look for a lyric analogue of plot in the progression or development of the poem's imagery.
>
> (*GM* 243)

Burke does so by analyzing Shelley's 'Ode to the West Wind'. The lyric is essentially a momentary lull in the action.

He goes on to instance Wordsworth's sonnet 'Composed Upon Westminster Bridge'. Crossing (the poem is set on a bridge) and incipience (it is morning) are not a preparation for action but parts of an intrinsic structure of *in*action:

> it is not the incipience of the internal debate, arrested at the moment of indecision prior to a decision from which grievous consequences are inevitably to follow. Nor is it a retrospective summary. It just *is*, a state of mind that has come to rest by reason of its summarizing nature. It encom-

passes. We are concerned not with its potentialities, but with it as an end in itself.... It envisions such rest as might be a ground, a beginning and end, of all action.

(*GM* 246)

If this is an example of the interpretative 'mode that stresses proportion of ingredients' (*PLF* 261), it is also surely essentializing rather than the opposite of essentializing. The deep calm the sonnet claims is synonymized and reasserted, at the expense of the contextualizing and negating elements that another reading might have stressed. That deep calm is itself won out of a negative construction, the poem begins on another, and it depends on stressing how untypical is its 'scene' – a depopulated city of smokeless air – to make its paradoxical and (for Wordsworth) unique claim for the superiority of the urban pastoral. Burke uses this to 'encompass' or 'summarize' his own argument for attitudes (or incipient actions) being complete in themselves. He has to do so however by omitting the poem's own distinctions, in favour of an interpretative distinction between the lyric as dramatic soliloquy and 'as an end in itself'. He makes the latter stress, a stress on lyric state rather than dramatic act. It is not then that the sonnet seems just to be a bad example for Burke's argument but that it reveals a failure of nerve in the argument itself. Through the notion of 'attitudes' Burke readmits a rhetoric of 'eloquence' rather than 'persuasion', of formal devices having no instrumental function. Literary language would then be recalcitrant to any more instrumental or functional sorts of explanation and in this sense would be analogous to non-verbal 'motion', to the events that exemplify an 'unanswerable opponent'. Even before its appendix, in which the pentad is supplemented by an alternative 'four master tropes', the *Grammar* contains a disruptive supplement to the rhetoric of substance and the dialectic of constitutions which would otherwise frame the argument. 'Attitudes' are 'the realm of "symbolic action" par excellence' and are embodied *par excellence* in the lyric poem. Burke's reading of the lyric is then no more than a series of assertions, a series of metonymic substitutions of a unitary and unarguable interpretation. It might seem then that the ambitions of Burke's project are no more than ambitions to extend the canon of New Critical interpretation.

This, I think, is not the case. The Wordsworth poem is made to summarize a case that remains supplementary to the argument of the *Grammar*. Margaret Schlauch's shrewd comment that Burke proceeds as though 'to accept' and 'to reject' were intransitive verbs is relevant in considering his remark that the Wordsworth poem 'encompasses'. An earlier comment, from '*The Philosophy of Literary Form*', provides the verb with its object:

> every document bequeathed us by history must be treated as a *strategy for encompassing a situation*. Thus, when considering some document like the American Constitution, we shall be automatically warned not to consider it in isolation, but as the *answer* or *rejoinder* to assertions current in the situation in which it arose. We must take this into account when confronting now the problem of abiding by its 'principles' in a situation that puts forth totally different questions than those prevailing at the time when the document was formed.
>
> (*PLF* 109)

Here the imperative to historicize is treated as congruent with the limits on interpretation in the present. Documents have a history in terms both of their production and of their continuing reception. To see them as interpretatively bounded by their 'origins' would be to falsify by omitting the whole second part of this history. On the other hand, to read them in isolation from this context would be to falsify by making them arbitrarily malleable to present needs. For good empirical reasons the United States Constitution can be said to have the functions more dubiously claimed for the Wordsworth lyric, to 'be a ground, a beginning and end, of all action' (*GM* 246).

A few sentences in *Attitudes Toward History* (134) become a lengthy footnote in *The Philosophy of Literary Form* (109–11 n. 26) which in turn gets transmuted into a seventy-page section of the *Grammar* (323–401) on the function of the Constitution. The United States Constitution is the fundamental juridical and ethical ground for all action there but, as Burke shows, this is not to say that it can be a wholly empirical test of his claims for action. Of course it is significant that Burke should return to this text. It is significant though not because it shows how interpretative 'principles' derived in 'theory' can be applied in 'practice'. The Constitution's arbitration of 'practice' is not such as to distinguish 'practice' from 'theory' at all. Rather, Burke will argue that the Constitution is an *act*. *The* Constitution as the grounds for interpretative appeals is inseparable from the apparently metaphysical notion of 'constitutions'. Burke sees in the term another term for 'grounds' or 'substance' and thus his discussion can instance at length his own 'substantival (motivational, or 'Constitutional') distinction between the human act and the physical event' (*GM* 368). Thus this section of the *Grammar* will be its 'representative anecdote'.

It is, we remember, an 'anecdote' which will provide the appropriate terminology for considering acts, while a 'calculus' is more appropriate for considering events. Thus the investigation of (the) 'Constitution' was the 'representative anecdote' with which the *Grammar* was to have begun; instead it comes near the end of the book proper, a meditation on beginnings, including on the beginning of the *Grammar* itself. The founding 'Constitution' is both a document and an idea. It is also a potential for constitution, the means of deriving 'is' from 'ought', and vice versa. As such, it will both exemplify and problematize the notion of the 'representative anecdote' itself: 'an anecdote, to be truly representative, must be synecdochic rather than metonymic; or, in other words, it must be a *part for the whole* rather than a *reduction of the mental to the physical*' (*GM* 326). This is a Coleridgean order of priorities. Burke wants to stress the 'representative' or 'typical' over the 'reductive' example. As he continues, 'if our theme were "communication", we should seek to form our terms about some typical instance of communication, rather than selecting some purely physical mode, as a highway system or telegraphic network' (*GM* 326). As such, the investigation of 'constitutions' can become, for Burke, a way of examining the symbolic contest of individual and collective interests which, as we have seen, is a major concern of the work of the thirties. This too is given a 'typical' example, or 'representative anecdote':

Even where the mood is so highly collectivistic as in the Americans' attachment to their local baseball team, we have but a vicarious or symbolic sociality here, since these teams are all privately owned businesses which but have the *mask* of public institutions.

(*GM* 395)

As this example suggests, the discussion can only end, once again, in a paradox which recognizes contingency. The paradox of federalism (*e pluribus unum*) is that on any given occasion a legislative (which is to say, an interpretative) body must determine whether to stress the unity or the diversity – either the interest of the nation as a whole or the right of an individual state to differ. There are of course many other interests represented by the Constitution, and though these may be incommensurate, the Constitution must support the rights of each – thus Burke later compares it with the Freudian id that 'knows no No' (*LSA* 68–9). On this level, what is 'typical' can only be what is seen to be interpreted similarly despite the near infinity of contingent circumstances. On the way to this familiar paradox much of Burke's contribution to rhetoric is summarized.

The United States Constitution is a document which requires continual reinterpretation because of appeals made to its grounding authority to authorize courses of action which its framers could never have foreseen. Thus it represents the 'rhetoric of substance', the discussion of which actually begins the *Grammar*. A constitution is representative of the way the apparently opposed terms 'substance' and 'motivation' are 'convertible': each can be exchanged for the other (*GM* 376). It is a founding, or substantival document which, as we have seen, means that it functions both as a beginning and as a terminal point. Thus the example of what is apparently most 'essential' furnishes an argument against essentialism. The Constitution is 'an enactment arising in history, hence a dialectical act' (*GM* 365). That is, though it necessarily has predictive ('potential') ambitions it is, also necessarily, directed towards particular, present ends: it has uses which are now in the past.

In other words, interpretation too is a dialectical act; it too is 'an enactment arising in history' to fulfil present needs. In this case, those are the needs of wartime. It is however the abnormal which defines the 'norm'. Burke has described the Constitution as 'a capitalist constitution'. In wartime the usual capitalist imperatives are reversed, not for the capitalist but for the worker. The worker is enjoined to individual sacrifice for the collective good, and enjoined to be a producer only and not also a consumer. Burke's own interpretative interests are evident here. He lets a counter-example stand in subsequent editions: 'In Russia we see evidence of an almost fanatical will to sacrifice as individuals in behalf of the public good – yet without the Hitlerite motive of booty. We know that this incentive derives from the collectivistic point of view' (GM 398). Well, now we know otherwise; but Burke's confident summary unwittingly supports his own argument about the relativity of interpretation. Constitutions are origins, but need to be acknowledged as such; and their power is in their justification of actions in the present. The dialectic of constitutions is then a historical dialectic: the Constitution must be seen to be changeable according to the competing interests that would interpret it and to circumstances to which it must 'respond' despite having occurred well in advance of them. Thus Burke quotes a newspaper column discussing a proposal that in the current emergency the forthcoming congressional elections be suspended – a suggestion which still has to seek for its essential grounding in the Constitution. Thus the Constitution must be changeable precisely in terms of its invariant or essential 'principles'. These must be determined by interpretation.

The 'principles' it represents may not be found embodied in the actual text of a constitution: it is up to a Court to determine 'principles' which it may infer from its spirit rather than finding them in its letter. That is to say, there is something (the Court continually decides) *beneath* the substance, *under* the grounds: 'the constitution-beneath-the-constitution':

> A Constitution is but a partial act; the only truly total act would be the act of a Supreme Founding Father who founded the Universal Substance, the Constitution-beneath-the-Constitution, the scene in which the constitution of 1789 was an enactment, and the motivational circumference of which extends far beyond the motives featured and encouraged by the local calculus that has formally governed our public relations for the last century and a half.
>
> (GM 374)

The Constitution needs to be grasped as a synecdoche and as an act. (These are from different terminologies, but they are the terminologies Burke veers between at the end of the *Grammar*.) Grasped as such, it can be seen continually to require the supplement of interpretation. For Burke it is Dramatism which can best align the act of production of a constitution (its historical uses) with functions it may be required to perform in the present.

There will then be differing versions of what is 'essential' – 'nineteenth-century thinking is one grand gallery of rival essentializations' (*GM*383). The participants in Burke's 'dialectic of constitutions' might be seen as two tendencies we have noted of his own discourse, the apparently opposed tendencies towards 'essentialism' and to 'perspective by incongruity'. The way these tendencies run together can be seen by running together two separate quotations from these pages where Burke deals with 'essentializing' arguments and with their apparent opposite:

> increasing complexity, giving rise to a compensatory cult of simplification, made 'essentializing' seem the most 'natural' mode of thought. 'It all boils down to this' ... etc. – an excellent direction in which to move, but a very bad one if arrived at by shortcuts ...
>
> Columnists, doing the Court's work in advance, have often made themselves highly serviceable in some quarters by ... essentializing and extrapolating the implications of some measure, which they feature in isolation, without reference to the modifying and corrective factors. It is the method used by all cartoonists to make us laugh; it is a method that can be used by our judges on and off the bench to make us tremble.
>
> (*GM* 383, 384)

The term 'perspective by incongruity' is not employed here, but it seems to be the method Burke describes in the second of these paragraphs. 'Perspective by incongruity', like the apparently opposite 'essentializing' movement, remains at the behest of an interested individual. Indeed, it might well be described as the kind of 'shortcut' Burke warns against in the first paragraph here. This would be a third usage of the trope, neither quite the response to perceived division nor the interpretative 'counter-statement' to a fallacious consensus or congruity. A constitution is 'representative' (standing for a large and diverse body of interests), and precisely because of this it requires from most of those whom it represents a vicarious participation, or no partic-ipation at all. What is crucial is the authority to be 'representative' invested in the interpreter. The constitution-beneath-the-constitution, the 'principle' isolated not just from what an article of the constitution says but from what it may not say, are *acts* of interpretation.[1]

We could stress that substance is an act, or that the act is substantial. Burke's Dramatism makes the first stress. In the *All-Area* interview he locates this stress in his debt to Aristotle:

> the line I got from Aristotle complicates my relation to the Kantian tradition, which builds around not action, but understanding. Aristotle's system was *ontological*, a theory of *being* (*being* as an act). Kant's was *epistemological*, rooted in a problem of *knowledge*. That's where I get my distinction between a 'dramatistic' and a 'scientistic' approach to thoughts on the human condition.
>
> (C-G 22)

In an article a few years later, the 'epistemological' half of this duality is ascribed not to 'science' but to his own 'Logology': ' "dramatism" and "logology" are analogous respectively to the traditional distinction (in theology and metaphysics) between ontology and epistemology ' (*DL* 89). It is puzzling to say the least that Burke should put the analogy this way round: if logology is concerned with the problem of knowledge, it is surely concerned with ultimate knowledge: that is, with ontol-ogy. Looking again at an argument cited in Chapter 2, this time from the perspective afforded by our consideration of Burke's techniques of the thirties, should show us the ways in which logology can return us to worldly problems.

Despite their comic strain, the stress upon a language of *social* action in *Permanence and Change* and *Attitudes Toward History* is a call for a massive shift in the dominant ideology. According to the utopian final act of the latter book's 'Curve of history', such a shift is imminent; yet the transition from 'Dramatism' to

'Logology' bespeaks a more restricted aim. Logology is a kind of essentialism that would go beyond theology and ontology to the essentially human, by locating the conditions for theology and ontology in the definitively human realm of language. Thus *The Rhetoric of Religion* can displace the Dramatistic terms 'action' and 'symbolic action' into 'matter' and 'essence'. We understand 'eternity', if at all, through understanding 'time', but neither can be understood outside the medium of language:

> there is one area in which we do experience ... in principle, the relation between 'time' and 'timelessness'. This is in the relation between the words of a sentence and its 'meaning'. The syllables of the words are 'born' and 'die'. But the *meaning* of those syllables 'transcends' their sheer nature as temporal motions. It is an *essence*, not reducible to any other part of the sentence, or even to the whole of it.
>
> (*RR* 142)

As often with Burke, it is not clear which side of the analogy – language or time? – has the priority here. What is clear is that 'symbolic action' points to another dimension (of 'meaning') which is separate from the sum of its linguistic parts:

> We must know what the words 'step aside' mean, if we are to obey them. But a push can have the same effect without our having to understand its 'meaning'. The push is material, 'temporal'; but the meaning of the words is in another dimension – and from the logological point of view the sheer materiality of a sentence is to this other dimension as 'time' is to 'timelessness'.
>
> (*RR* 143)

The gesture towards mysticism or metaphysics here actually shows where the priority lies in the analogy: the final concern of 'logology' is with words; 'theology' here is only its object of study. Elsewhere in the book the direction is clearer: Burke is concerned, he says, with the 'reclamation and refurbishment' of theological terms (*RR* 190), and in reclaiming and refurbishing words for a world of contingency, division, negation and distinctions he brings verbal action not to rest in a norm but to a continual reciprocity. The critique of origins implicit in a 'dialectic of Constitutions' uncovers contradictions, but this does not gainsay the empirical authority of a Constitution in the present. The 'unanswerable opponent' of the title-essay of *The Philosophy of Literary Form* requires to be answered not only in its own terms, but dialectically, by exposure of the relationship between essential and contingent realms. Thus in the *Rhetoric of Motives*, after asserting the priority of the ideal (the capacity to use symbols) 'to any *particular* property structure' (*RM* 136), Burke states such a dialectical method to be indispensable to any interpretation that would be 'creative':

> a way of living and thinking is reducible to terms of an 'idea' – and that 'idea' will be 'creative' in the sense that anyone who grasps it will embody it or represent it in any mode of action he may choose. The idea, or underlying principle, must be approached by him through the sensory images of his cultural scene. But until he intuitively grasps the principle of such an imaginal clutter, he cannot be profoundly creative, so far as the genius of that 'idea' is concerned. For to be profoundly representative of a culture, he will imitate not its mere insignia, but the principle behind the *ordering* of those insignia.
>
> (*RM* 137)

In asserting the dialectical relationship, Burke repeats the contradiction alluded to at the start of this chapter: 'creative' acts of interpretation may well have the end of securing an identity with an 'idea, or underlying principle', but an individual may surely 'embody' or 'represent' such a principle passively and without knowing that s/he does so. Representativeness or embodiment might only be discernible to an interpreter, and that interpreter might be committed neither to the 'sensory images' of the culture nor to the idea to which they can be reduced. Thus the confused voluntarism of human agency has to be trumped by the voluntarism of the idea – an idea that is personified at the start of this quotation, in a Hegelian way, as itself a creative actor which is immanent in the images of a culture. Thus 'identification' names the ways in which we can, as it were, act upon or persuade ourselves (*DD* 28). Of course this solution too leads to circularity (the idea creates images which are images of itself); but the circularity permits a reciprocal, dialectical movement which privileges neither the essential idea nor the continual succession of instances in which the contingent breaks in upon it to re-present this idea.

I am not trying to dignify confusion by naming it 'dialectic' (the name for a practice which seems historically to have succeeded rhetoric, a succession of which Plato, in the *Gorgias* and *Phaedrus*, is the genealogist). The passage quoted above seems to me both a provisional solution to, and an example of the central problem of Burke's project. Having approached it 'empirically' through his extended example of the Constitution, I want now to approach it more 'theoretically' through Burke's attempt to describe the priorities and transformations involved in any interpretation of language. The reconciliation of opposites, in Coleridge's phrase, depends first of all on identifying the terms of an opposition, in the sense of contextually or dialectically defining terms, before they can be identified, this time in the sense of bringing them together, of reconciling them. This last, ethical aim is what Burke takes to be the aim of his rhetoric.

The incipient Dramatism of *The Philosophy of Literary Form* is a theory 'got by treating the terms "dramatic" and "dialectical" as synonymous' (*PLF* xx), but Plato's dialectic is a means always of persuading Socrates' interlocutor to acknowledge truths that are already known to Socrates. Burke's sense of dialectic is rather what I earlier called homeopathic: 'All enterprises are dialectical which would cure us through the medium of words – and all the more so if their words would cure us by training us in the distrust of words' (*GM* 240). As he says earlier of psychoanalysis: 'The cure must bear notable affinities with the disease: all effective medicines are potential poisons' (*PC* 126). Nevertheless the metaphor of a cure implies that dialectic can be a course or method of treatment amounting to a remedy, as error is remedied in the Platonic dialogues. To be cured is to be in a new state of certainty, if only of a negative certainty that a disease is now absent. Later in the *Grammar*, there is a definition of dialectic as a method whose end is less certain, or in which certainty is impossible: 'By dialectics in the most general sense we mean the employment of the possibilities of linguistic transformation'

(*GM* 402). Here 'transformation', unlike 'cure', does not involve a single state: things are transformed from one state to another but will also be in some intervening state or states of transformation. The dialectical 'cure' of words by words may result not in certainty but in the process by which ambiguities become codified as either 'merger' or 'division', in further transformations. Whether 'division' is a symptom of historical conditions for which there is no cure, or whether its rhetorical counterpart in 'merger' can have its end in a newly ethical condition, the consideration of transformations remains the crucial problematic of Burke's project. It is, for example, the import of his 'dialectic of constitutions'.

The crucial moments of transformation in Burke's history are moments of linguistic transformation:

> The great departures in human thought can be eventually reduced to a moment where the thinker treats as *op*posite, key terms formerly considered *ap*posite, or *v.v.* So we are admonished to be on the look-out for those moments when strategic synonymizings or desynonymizings occur. And, in accordance with the logic of our ratios, when they do occur, we are further admonished to be on the look-out for a shift in the source of derivation, as terms formally derived from different sources are now derived from a common source, or *v.v.*
>
> (*GM* 192)

'Synonymizings or desynonymizings' are terms from Coleridge to which we shall return in a moment; but what is important here (for all that it is acknowledged as an eventual reduction) is that Burke locates a crucial transformation in a linguistic division. (He is discussing the empirical–transcendental division in Kant.)

The *Grammar* begins with 'substance'. Near its end, in a section on 'merger' and 'division', it anticipates the *Rhetoric*'s focus on 'identification' in its hints of 'consubstantiality'. Extremes meet, and agreement on a 'common ground' of 'values', though it permits (and may even require) oppositions, limits the possibility of opposition to terms occurring on that ground. Burke gives the example of *Othello*:

Iago may be considered 'consubstantial' with Othello in that he represents the principles of jealousy implicit in Othello's delight in Desdemona as a private spiritual possession. Iago, to arouse Othello, must talk a language that Othello knows as well as he, a language implicit in the nature of Othello's love as the idealization of his private property in Desdemona. This language is the dialectical opposite of Othello's; but it so thoroughly shares a common ground with Othello's language that its insinuations are never for one moment irrelevant to Othello's thinking. Iago must be cautious in leading Othello to believe them as *true*: but Othello never for a moment doubts them as *values*.

(GM 414)

What becomes crucial here then, as in 'the great departures in human thought', is the points at which divisions occur. As Burke summarizes:

The strategic choice between synonymizing and desynonymizing ... momentously affects a writer's key terms. For we may stress either the element that two terms have in common or those respects wherein they are distinct. And if they are ancestral terms, different perspectives may be generated from such beginnings, as a slight deflection at the centre may show as a vast one at the circumference.

(GM 414)

The theoretical summary of the import of the 'representative anecdote' can lead us to the final text I want to discuss.

Burke's introduction to *A Grammar of Motives* provides, among other things, a rationale for what has seemed to some the idiosyncracy of his own terminology by claiming as the province of his work the terminology of presupposition, deceit and desire which constitutes 'motives'. Given the historical scene in which his work was produced – or, in essentialist terms, the Babel which human beings inhabit – this terminology will be inevitably ambiguous and inconsistent: 'Accordingly, what we want is *not terms that avoid ambiguity*, but *terms that clearly reveal the strategic spots at which ambiguities necessarily arise*' (GM xviii).

Thus titular terms such as those for philosophic schools, a taxonomy of which occupies the bulk of the *Grammar*, must be particularly prone to ambiguity, since grouping any phenomena together under a title implies a judgement that the variations among them are relatively unimportant. For Burke, both the titles and the variations they suppress will be linguistic. To employ terms from a passage already quoted, transformations occur at 'moments when strategic synonymizings or desynonymizings occur' (*GM* 192).

The terms are drawn from Coleridge who, in the fourth chapter of *Biographia Literaria*, first adumbrates a famous distinction: the distinction of 'imagination' from 'fancy':

> in all societies there exists an instinct of growth, a certain collective unconscious good sense working progressively to desynonymize those words originally of the same meaning which the conflux of dialects had supplied to the more homogeneous languages, as the Greek and German, and which the same cause, joined with accidents of translation from original works of different countries, occasion in mixt languages like our own. The first and most important point to be proved is that two conceptions perfectly distinct are confused under one and the same word, and (this done) to appropriate that word exclusively to one meaning, and the synonyme (should there be one) to the other. But if (as will be often the case in the arts and sciences) no synonyme exists, we must either invent or borrow a word.
>
> (Coleridge 1983: I, 82–4)

This certainly suggests a project of linguistic 'reclamation and refurbishment' (*RR* 190) which Burke claims also to be his. Likewise, the appeal here to a collective and consensual linguistic genius finds echoes in Burke's confidence in a ' "folk criticism" ' (*PLF* 301; *ATH* 173). However, Coleridge almost at once qualifies his apparent confidence in such a resource by a lengthy footnote in which it is clear that the 'collective unconscious good sense' is instigated by an individual thinker:

> When two distinct meanings are confounded under one or more words (and such must be the case, as sure as our

knowledge is progressive and of course imperfect), erroneous consequences will be drawn, and what is true in the sense of the word will be affirmed as true *in toto*. Men of research, startled by the consequences, seek in the things themselves (whether in or out of the mind) for a knowledge of the fact, and having discovered the difference remove the equivocation either by the substitution of a new word or by the appropriation of one of the two or more words that had before been used promiscuously. When this distinction has been so naturalized and of such general currency that the language itself does as it were *think* for us (like the sliding rule which is the mechanic's safe substitute for arithmetical knowledge) we then say that it is evident to *common sense*. Common sense, therefore, differs in different ages.

(Coleridge 1983: I, 86)

I have quoted these passages at length to demonstrate the similarity not only of their concerns but also of their whole idiom to Burke's, and I simply want to draw out some of their implications because I think the similarity continues, and continues to be significant. Burke, like Coleridge, posits language in a state prior to division. Neither posits this state nostalgically; each tries to account for the 'growth' evident in a language. Language is organic for Coleridge, and can indeed be personified: only such metaphors can account for the simultaneous presence within a language of new terminological distinctions and of older ambiguities. For Coleridge, philosophical innovation comes from making distinctions in language. It is the role of the philosopher both to instigate and to follow the organic movement of 'desynonymizing' on which the progress of a society itself depends. (Only the first of these imperatives is evident here, but both are expressed by Coleridge elsewhere.)[2] The relativism of 'common sense' alluded to at the end of this passage at least allows Coleridge to attack what he takes to be the ideological laxity of the common sense of his immediately post-war world. It also admits a tension though. The progress of a language, and hence of a society, may come primarily from an original thinker or from common language, but must come primarily from one or the other. All these themes are suggested in Burke's use of the Coleridgean terms. The introduction to *A Grammar of Motives* continues with a passage in which 'ambiguity' is posited not as a site of problems which are to be resolved but as a necessary effect of the linguistic 'substance' from which transformation can occur. Here 'grounds' are in flux, molten:

> Distinctions, we might say, arise out of a great central moltenness, where all is merged. They have been thrown from a liquid center to the surface, where they have congealed. Let one of these crusted distinctions return to its source, and in this alchemic center it may be remade, again becoming molten liquid, and may enter into new combinations, whereat it may be again thrown forth as a new crust, a different distinction. So that A may become non-A. But not merely by a leap from one state to another. Rather, we must take A back into the ground of its existence, the logical substance that is its causal ancestor, and on to a point where it is consubstantial with non-A; then we may return, this time emerging with non-A instead.
>
> (*GM* xix)

Certainly there is here a defence of the seeming arbitrariness of Burke's terminology – a defence based on the necessary arbitrariness of any interpretative terminology – but this remarkable passage is more than just a defence by analogy. Here the 'ground' or 'substance' of linguistic distinctions is envisaged as primal, amorphous stuff. It is stuff which seems at first to contain potential 'motion' like magma, then to contain potential 'action' like molten lead in the alchemist's alembic. Remembering the contradictions of the Coleridge passages though, we would have to say that this seems to be alchemy without an alchemist. The action by which distinctions are formed and then melt seems to be an act without an agent, to be self-motivated. Language does not only 'as it were *think* for us' but also acts without us. Coleridge's contradictory sketch for a sociology of language is essentialized by Burke as a metaphysic of language. An agent for these actions, a grammatical subject that is not reflexive, appears only in the final sentence of this passage, and it is Burke's characteristic authorial 'we'. The narrator's pronoun, that is, generalizes the action in which it is now revealed to be participating. This action can therefore be seen as necessary, as an imperative for interpretation. Furthermore, it can be seen as the reverse of Coleridge's 'desynonymization'. Terms apparently distinct must first be 'synonymized'. They must be returned to the 'ancestor' with which they can be shown to be 'consubstantial'. Only by such a labour of the negative can the interpreter re-emerge with usably distinctive terms.

Although this last suggests a metaphor for interpretation as archaeology (or even as deep-sea diving), the metaphor from alchemy on which this passage is based suggests a reason why Burke's work has been received with hostility, where it has been received, or not taken seriously. Far from reassuring us about the idiosyncracy of his terminology, such a metaphor might lead us to see that idiosyncracy as final: to see Burke as conjuring a system which cannot possibly be exemplary because it is not only hermetic but also hermetically sealed. For instance, in republishing his essay on Burke Fredric Jameson follows it with an earlier-written essay in which at one point Burke is compared unfavourably to Hayden White by means of a dismissal of the former's 'alchemy':

> White's synthesis ... does not suffer from the hubris of his great predecessor and model Kenneth Burke, whose work strikes us in retrospect as a kind of monstrous bricolage designed for the production of nothing less than the philosopher's stone itself.
>
> (Jameson 1988: 156)

Jameson's infection by Burke's metaphor here might itself be argued to be evidence for Burke's Coleridgean claim that language can 'as it were *think* for us' – that metaphor, rather than being in a fixed relation to 'reality', takes on independently discursive functions. Nevertheless, it *is* Burke's metaphor, suggesting that Dramatism will be a mystifying pseudo-science of transformations and the search for a universal essence grounding all of them. This of course has not been my argument. There are elements like this in Burke's writings, and they should not be seen merely as deplorable elements which, when only disposed of, leave us with a working, imitable model free of the contingencies under which it was composed and the disabling 'style' of its author. Coleridge too is often read in this way, a way which can take us to Jameson's view of Burke that one of the greatest of our totalizing critics is: Kenneth Burke, *hélas*.

What we have been considering is, after all, a metaphor for distinction and transformation. Burke reminds us that 'the test of a metaphor's validity ... require[s] nothing less than the *filling-out, by concrete body, of the characterizations which one would test'*, and that the test is determined by the metaphor that is most inclusive (*PLF*, 145). A metaphor for Burke may be prospective – a way of predicting phenomena that have not yet occurred – as well as being a retrospective abstraction from phenomena. Essentialist terms like 'grounds' or 'substance' are metaphors of this kind. If metaphor is not simply parallel to the literal, a kind of metarealism, nor is it, in turn, simply a set of transformations of a wholly nominal reality. A metaphor may be said to partake of both essence and phenomenon, and is to be 'tested' by shuttling between these. Burke recommends reading his own work in this dialectical manner, a recommendation already implicit in the discussions of aesthetic form in the earlier work, and particularly in the claim that form is a means of 'orientation'. A passage in *Counter-Statement* suggests that the medium of such orientation is necessarily metaphor:

> we can continue to discuss a subject only by taking up in turn various aspects of it. (Recalling the schoolmen's subdivisions of a topic: *quis, quid, ubi, quibus auxiliis, cur, quo modo, quando*. One talks about a thing by talking about something else.) We establish a direction by co-ordinates; we establish a curve by three points, and thereupon can so place other points that they will be intercepted by this curve. Thus, though forms need not be prior to experience, they are certainly prior to the work of art exemplifying them.
>
> (*CS* 141)

Here the parenthesis anticipates the terms of the later *Grammar*, which are themselves metaphors. In a footnote to *The Rhetoric of Religion* there is the reminder that the terms of the pentad are interrogative rather than positive and 'are really but a set of *blanks to be filled out*. They are an algebra, not an arithmetic' (*RR* 26); and, in the addendum to the University of California Press edition of the *Grammar*, there is the remark that 'all the ratios are essentially analogies' (*GM* 444). Burke's interpretative terms then are not the reified terms of an interpretative grid but are metaphors for transformation, and can themselves be transformed. This is not to blame Burke again for being a conjurer (this time perhaps a Prospero) but to praise the flexibility of his methodology. This enjoins agility on the interpreter too. Burke's writings are exemplary, but not because they furnish a method to be repeated and illustrated. They offer a methodology rather than a method. Diagnoses of our postmodern condition may imply that interpretation is exhausted; but reports of its death have been greatly exaggerated: actually, it is again in crisis. Asked if he was a postmodernist, Burke replied, 'I hope not', and his eclecticism, his allusiveness, his cheerful assumption of the availability of all western thought (all of which are traits of postmodernist thinking), are always attended by an insistence that thought is an action in and upon history, a history which includes the present. Shifts of stress, translations and substitutions are the rhetorical transformations necessary for a methodology – a rhetoric – which would be adequate to objects of interpretation which only become such by being contextualized in one among a near infinity of ways. Burke is not a relativist because such contextualization necessarily occurs in any act of interpretation. The charge that could more justly be made against him is rather that his methodology is too generous: in allowing differences to complicate any interpretative model, differences themselves can be melted, liquefied. In moving from the abstraction of a model that describes how verbal distinctions emerge to models in which the terms are a site of present ideological contest Burke can assume that those terms actually behave, or should behave, as they do in the essentialist metaphor. This can be called generous because it seems again and again to be the product of a liberal and comic impulse. To use some terms from Coleridge again: the wider the scope of a particular term or set of terms the greater the likelihood of transforming division into mere distinction. We may not share Burke's optimism on this point, but there is an unsentimental generosity in his contending it. He contends that 'symbolic action' is not an escape from but, precisely, a symbolization of conflicts, a means of acting upon history rather than being acted upon. Burke's project stresses action rather than knowledge; in the fifties he describes it as motivated by a 'humanitarian concern to see how far conflict (war) may be translated practically into linguistic struggle and how such verbal struggle may be made to eventuate in a common enactment short of physical combat' (LAPE 268).

Conclusion: strategies

This book has argued that Kenneth Burke's kind of interpretation provides cultural studies with an urgent example. I want to conclude by returning to some of the ways in which he has been read in order to claim that Burke offers a methodology which still remains to be exploited. So I refer to cultural studies because of the inadequacy of considering Burke solely or even principally as a literary critic. Rather than summarizing the arguments of his work I want first of all to return to some of the negative claims made about it: for example that it fails to engage with the terms of debate current in any of the disciplines on which it encroaches and that it overvalues metaphor and arguments from analogy at the expense of logic.

Burke was born nearly a hundred years ago. His vocabulary can seem not only idiosyncratic but also anachronistic. The terms against which he defines his own terms can now seem quaint rather than sinister: a choice between 'aestheticism' and 'behaviourism' doesn't look like a very urgent choice. It was Burke who first translated Thomas Mann's *novellen* into English and who pasted up *The Waste Land* for its first American publication in *The Dial*, while his dependence upon essentialist arguments, his conviction of the basic rationality and benevolence of human behaviour, together with the holistic ambitions of his theory as a whole, can make him seem uncomfortably pre-modern. His project was to make a theory of language – more broadly, of symbolic action – which could account for the limits of a given linguistic situation and also for the discursive changes within which they were set. This is a project which, even if it seems heroic, seems heroic like Don Quixote was heroic. It can be charged with being repetitive, with depending on analogy rather than logic, with announcing 'principles' derived from analysis as though they had generated the analysis, and perhaps with mistaking American liberalism for 'human nature'; but these constitute not failings in the project but some of its most important insights. Rather than being exceptional, aberrant instances of discourse these are the unconscious strategies of discourse itself.

'Strategies' is a word Burke translates from a military to a rhetorical context.[1] As a metaphor, the word retains traces of its original context and hovers between action and symbolic action. (If we're unsympathetic to Burke we would say that it dignifies the retrospective, secondary and derived nature of interpretation with associations of mortal consequence.) To say that discourse can employ 'strategies' is to personify discourse, turning it from something that can be used into something that can use itself. Rhetorically, this is prosopopoeia, the figure by which inanimate objects speak, and it is the figure Coleridge nervously employs when he suggests that 'language itself does as it were *think* for us'. We speak with less discomfort of, say, 'the ideology of texts' though in doing so we are doing something rhetorically similar. We feel more comfortable with such a locution, I suggest, because of an unconscious suspicion, however it may be consciously denied, that textual meanings originate in and may be foreclosed by the author of that text. That is, we are more comfortable with the notion of a text or discourse having an 'ideology' than with its employing 'strategies' because the former can assign meaning to an author, not agency to an inanimate object. With a text whose authorship is anonymous or collective (proverbs, the US Constitution, 'history') we can again feel more comfortable with generalized notions of 'its' ideology; alternatively, we may feel that to so generalize is to be an idiot and that the business of interpretation is with particulars. Although strategies may then be attributed to a reader rather than to her text, such an attribution would commit us not to honorific particularity but to hopeless relativism since we could no longer appeal to the text to validate the claims we made about it.

The martial associations of the term 'strategy' are to do with directing a campaign rather than a battle. A field commander in

108

the presence of the enemy employs tactics. A strategy is rather the set of such operations, the logic they follow. It is evident that this may be a logic that can only be discerned retrospectively, and that strategies may need to be modified in the light of the contingent and the unexpected. A strategy has both a spatial aspect – the deployment of available resources – and a temporal or narrative aspect – those resources are deployed in sequence. The presence of an opponent anticipating your strategies and initiating their own, together with variables such as the weather, means that a strictly causal logic is likely only to be apparent once a sequence is complete. Spatial and temporal dimensions may be separated for purposes of analysis – as with Saussure's distinction of 'synchronic' from 'diachronic' linguistics – but a full description must involve both: hence the yoking together of these two dimensions in Burke's title *A Grammar of Motives*. Burke does provide the 'active categories' he calls for in the 'Literature as equipment for living' essay (*PLF* 303). Provided we accept the validity of arguments from analogy in the first place, 'strategies' may then be a good analogy for the description of any reasonably extended piece of language and an exact one for the highly motivated and organized language of literary texts or for the adversarial rhetoric of political ones. The advantage of such a term is that it enables us to see what I have called a 'system' or 'project' as active. Its disadvantage is that we may be led into a territory in which the duality of text and reader and of the metaphorical and literal may be elided. This, as we have seen, is the territory of theology. Kenneth Burke is however a reader in Babel and is only ever momentarily nostalgic for Eden.

This book has treated him as an exemplary reader. It has considered Burke as a rhetorician and as an ideological critic. These terms are not synonymous but Burke demonstrates that to regard rhetoric and ideology as wholly discrete realms is to be in thrall to both. Burke's own objection to the term ideology being applied to his work is an objection to what he takes to be a single, specialized discourse, the economic, taking priority over an essentialist definition of human beings themselves. Burke himself does not always employ the term 'ideology' in the crude sense which leads him finally to reject it; but in retreating from the term he is led to employ several alternative terms ('value', 'attitude' and 'motive' itself) for the functions which it names. He is equally suspicious of a determinate 'history', and the early work gleefully provides alternate versions. Actually it is 'rhetoric' which is the more troublesome term. In part this is because rhetoric is both a practice and the study of that practice: the latter hypostasizes an object of study which is outside itself. Periodically the fraught relation between words and actions becomes attenuated – which is to say that rhetoric treats it as such and comes to see its task as being intrinsically verbal and descriptive. Where Burke's texts have been read, there have been attempts to assimilate them to this kind of rhetoric.

Describing Burke as a rhetorician and as an ideological critic suggests why it is inadequate to consider him only alongside mid-twentieth century literary critics and to regard him for good or ill as a road not taken. His argument with the American New Critics was not an argument over the interpretation of particular texts and nor was it an argument over interpretative methods but over the methodology governing interpretation. (They appealed to Aristotle but Burke showed that they needed to take their Aristotle whole.) More recently, he has been suggested as a figure who can heal the current breach between textualist and contextualist modes of literary interpretation. Where Burke has been taken up in America it has been by and large in departments of 'speech' and 'rhetoric' where his career is often taken as a *vade mecum*, as an example of how the beguilements of Marxism might be avoided, and where his rhetoric can be accommodated to the phenomenology of texts. The argument of this book has been that Burke is most exemplary not as an interpreter of 'literary' texts but as a reader of proverbs, of constitutions, of the narrative of 'history' itself. There are local gains to be had from Burke's kind of interpretation but these local instances are synecdoches, part of the bigger gains to be had from the way (often surprising) they can be contextualized. Reading proverbs leads him to announce a 'sociological criticism'; he moves from the Constitution to constitutions; and he writes not history but historiography.

The argument is not that the general must be superior to the particular. To synonymize those nouns as the collective and the individual may make the point that what is involved is an ideological and not merely an epistemological choice. The point is raised in the course of an astute essay by Angus Fletcher which also has a bearing on the question raised in the introduction of why the reception of Burke should have been almost entirely in America. At one point Fletcher's essay compares Burke with a critic he admires, William Empson:

> Empson's large subject, which is traditionally English, is the class struggle. Burke's is the typically American subject: the struggle of man as an individual to survive in a world that is not, *ab initio*, limited by accepted, national, traditional, or even class lines of demarcation.... He's a bit like Walt Whitman, who besides singing of himself, sang of everything else he could think of.
>
> (Fletcher 1982: 157)

The comment is intuitively right, and generous if condescending to what someone called the 'Yankee Crank' in Burke. The antithesis is attractive but distorts Burke's writing by turning Burke's dreams and nightmares of western 'order' into the American dream. The 'typically American subject' to which Burke supposedly contributes is one in which the individual simply overwrites the forces that would determine others. Not to see 'struggle' (Fletcher's term) as ideological can look less like heroic refusal than like wilful blindness. Burke is not an(other) American Adam, just as he is not Robinson Crusoe. He does have his *ab initio* definitions but the very contexts in which they are offered insist that such definitions are always rhetorically belated and are reached from within circumstances in which limitations, contests, arguments are already active. As Burke himself aphoristically expressed this dialectical fate: 'The driver drives the car, but the traffic drives the driver' (WS 311).[2]

We can now grasp the extent to which, on his own and years ago, Burke was pursuing arguments which, later and in others, excited us by their novelty. It would be equally mistaken though to find in Burke merely an anticipation and thus a confirmation of the present. Certainly he does anticipate many of the concerns that have dominated Anglo-American theory since the late sixties. Indeed, the notion of 'theory' itself – a study which does not seek validation from a particular object of study but which still does not get taken seriously by the philosophers – is anticipated in Burke's practice. He shows the inadequacy of the

111

commonsensical opposition of 'theory' to 'practice'. His theory of literary forms as forms of symbolic action, many of which have counterparts in the realm of action, suggests ways of reading both. He reads and encourages us to read analogically rather than allegorically: such reading discovers not a realm of archetypes but the rhetorical similarities between texts and events apparently dissimilar in content. This for example suggests a kind of structuralist enterprise. Some of Burke has affinities with the formulaic 'demystification' of the myths of consumer society in the Roland Barthes of *Mythologies*, but Burke refuses to be satisfied with what can be the mere panache of 'demystification' (his 'debunking'). Mystery is something re-current or essential; after the death of the gods it is manifest in social forms – and so it was, Burke would add, when the gods were still alive.

The last chapter ended with Burke's critique of the ways in which our actions and specifically our 'symbolic actions' can be shown to rest on grounds which themselves are discovered to be acts. While there may be consolation there could be little satisfaction in such discoveries. There would be a wholly unus-able paradox in regarding as a point of rest the discovery that the fixity which apparently guarantees action is itself unfixed, unstable. In taking us to a logical impasse Burke can also lead us out. Rather than beginning and ending in the necessary limitations upon any interpretative act we can move outwards from the equally necessary proximity of an act of interpretation to other acts of interpretation and to other acts in general. Of course we may take the logical impasse with us as we move outwards but, as the term 'strategies' demonstrates, such recon-textualizations may in turn be a means of discovering a logical impasse within the discourses studied. Burke shows how con-stitutions have continually to be substantiated by reference to a prior constitution. This is just as true of a constitution like that of the United States which builds 'upgrades' into the originating system. The stability of new orders may depend upon abandon-ing the old while appealing to its precedent, and 'priority' is a term which may disguise the hierarchical with the temporal. Idiosyncrasy and incongruity thus become ways of discovering the 'planned incongruities' by which states have ideologically constituted themselves. As Paul Kenny puts it: 'Speculatively detached from the determinate forms of political science, Burke's invention of "dramatism" was a way of getting back into its constitution without agreeing to its clauses' (Kenny 1992: 59).

The *Grammar of Motives* depends on ratios, on contexts which though conceivably infinite in number are each reductive and determinate – that is, explanatory. Burke's rhetoric is practised in the area between a determinate vocabulary and the contexts in which such a vocabulary has been or might be employed, between the scene and the 'variety of circumferences' within which it is constructed (*GM* 84). Burke calls the realm that the *Grammar* will study 'the Human Barnyard', but that realm is two realms always impinging on each other. The realms of action and symbolic action are separate but analogous. Neither realm is conceived of as static, each is a version of the contest being fought in the other; each is as much market-place as barnyard. Behind these realms we can seem to glimpse an 'unanswerable opponent'. Burke's example is to make it answerable.

Notes

Introduction

1 The quotation is from the interview with J. Hillis Miller in Saluszinsky 1987: 224. This is a softer version of the argument which would appropriate Burke not as a forerunner of but as an alternative to a hydra called 'deconstruction'. See for example Southwell (1987). Other versions of Burke sketched (or caricatured) here will be considered later in this introduction.

1 Equipment for living

1 The anecdote is recounted by Herb Simons, *Kenneth Burke Society Newsletter*, vol. II, no. 1 (July 1986), 1. Simons repeats the anecdote in his 'Introduction: Kenneth Burke and the rhetoric of the human sciences', to Melia and Simons (1989), 23.

See also the opening of Burke's story ' The anaesthetic revelation of Herone Liddell', in *The Complete White Oxen: Collected Short Fiction of Kenneth Burke* (Berkeley: University of California Press, 1968).

2 A god coming down to earth

1 see C 327, and this revision:

Man is
the symbol-using (symbol-making, symbol-misusing) animal
inventor of the negative (or moralized by the negative)
separated from his natural condition by instruments of his own making
goaded by the spirit of hierarchy (or moved by the sense of order)
and rotten with perfection.

(*LSA* 16)

A footnote in *RR* expands this to: ' The animal that makes, uses, and misuses symbols' (*RR* 42), and there are others subsequently.

115

2 Burke wants to keep the literal and metaphorical apart and to stress that his Dramatism is literal. This stress requires a binary term, an opposite that can be metaphorical, and Burke persists in casting in this role ' behaviourism'. In his reply to Wayne Booth he asks Booth to

> note that in my *Encyclopaedia* article, I fight valiantly for the claim that 'Dramatism', as a model, *is not a metaphor*, but literal; and Behaviorism, with its view of man as *in essence* a machine rather than as a symbol using animal subject to mechanistic frailties, is the figurative approach to things concerned with human motivation.
>
> (Booth 1979: 133)

3 'God-term' is defined in *RR* 2–3.
4 It is also a verbatim repetition of the section on 'The representative anecdote', *GM* 59. Burke can simply repeat the formulation of twenty years earlier.

3 The spiritual counterpart of roadways

1 I suspect here that Burke has in mind Dr J. Robert Oppenheimer, with whom he worked at the Institute for Advanced Study at Princeton and who is acknowledged at the start of the *Rhetoric* (*RM* viii).
2 See Booth (1979).

4 This alchemic centre

1 The logological counterpart of this 'Dramatistic' insight occurs in the lengthy section 'The First Three Chapters of Genesis' in *The Rhetoric of Religion* where the original constitutive term is the 'Covenant'. History begins in the Covenant between God and the Israelites. However, prior to this is the Creation. The 'in the beginning' of Genesis offers itself as 'the constitution-beneath-the-constitution', prefiguring the Covenant, as explained by the commentaries. Second, the constitutive term 'Covenant' needs to be substituted by a term that can be negated, because the point about a Covenant is that it can be and will be broken (*RR* 179–81).
2 See Coleridge (1949: 152, 174), and for an argument taking Coleridge's claims for 'desynonymy' as central to what can be seen as a radical project in which meaning can be possessed by a community, see Hamilton (1983).

The Romantic provenance suggested for Burke's argument for meaning here is not accidental. Compare Shelley's *Defence of Poetry*:

> Every original language near to its source is in itself the chaos of a cyclic poem; the copiousness of lexicography and the

distinctions of grammar are the works of a later age and are
merely the catalogue and the form of the creations of poetry.
(Shelley 1988: 279)

The metaphysic of poetry suggested here is in Burke's version a
metaphysic of language as a whole. I have quoted Coleridge's
version because it allows, as Burke's does, for the social agency of
such a power.

Conclusion: strategies

1 He claims to be the first to do so, but the 1987 supplement to the *OED*
   cites a 1944 usage of the singular form from game theory and adds
   the following definition: 'In (theoretical) circumstances of competition or conflict, as in the theory of games, decision theory, business
   administration, etc., a plan for successful action based on the rationality and interdependence of the moves of the opposing
   participants.'
2 Characteristically prophesying after the event, the piece from which
   this is quoted appears three years after publication of Burke's satire
   ' Towards Helhaven: three stages of a vision', *Sewanee Review*, 79
   (1971), 11–25, to which it is a preface.

References

Anderson, Perry (1976) *Considerations on Western Marxism* (London: New Left Books).

Booth, Wayne C. (1979) 'The multiplication of perspectives', in *Critical Understanding: The Powers and Limits of Pluralism* (Chicago: University of Chicago Press), 98–137.

Coleridge, Samuel Taylor (1949) *The Philosophical Lectures of Samuel Taylor Coleridge*, ed. Kathleen Coburn (London: Pilot Press).

— —(1983) *Biographia Literaria*, ed. James Engell and Walter Jackson Bate, 2 vols; vol. 7 of *The Collected Works of S. T. Coleridge*, (London: Routledge and Kegan Paul; Princeton, NJ: Princeton University Press).

Dowling, William C. (1984) *Jameson, Althusser, Marx: an Introduction to The Political Unconscious* (London: Methuen).

Eagleton, Terry (1991) *Ideology: an Introduction* (London: Verso).

Eliot, T. S. (1934) 'William Blake', in *Selected Essays*, 2nd edn, revised (London: Faber), 317–22. First published in 1920.

Feehan, Michael (1979) 'Kenneth Burke's discovery of dramatism', *Quarterly Journal of Speech*, 65: 405–11.

Fletcher, Angus (1982) 'Volume and body in Burke's criticism', in White and Brose (1982), 150–75.

Gusfield, Joseph R. (ed. and intro.) (1989a) *Kenneth Burke on Symbols and Society*, Heritage of Sociology Series (Chicago and London: University of Chicago Press).

— —(1989b) 'The bridge over separated lands: Kenneth Burke's significance for the study of social action', in Melia and Simons (1989), 28–54.

Hamilton, Paul (1983) *Coleridge's Poetics* (Oxford: Basil Blackwell).

Hartman, Geoffrey (1980) *Criticism in the Wilderness: the Study of Literature Today* (New Haven and London: Yale University Press).

Henderson, Greig E. (1988) *Kenneth Burke: Literature and Language as Symbolic Action* (Athens, Ga.: University of Georgia Press).

Jameson, Fredric (1978a) 'Symbolic inference; or, Kenneth Burke and ideological analysis', *Critical Inquiry* vol. 4, no. 3 (Spring 1978), 507–23, also in White and Brose (1982), 68–91.

119

— — (1978b) 'Critical response II: ideology and symbolic action' *Critical Inquiry* vol. 5, no. 2 (Winter 1978), 417–22.

— — (1981) *The Political Unconscious: Narrative as a Socially Symbolic Act* (Ithaca, NY: Cornell University Press).

— — (1988) *Situations of Theory*, vol. 1 of *The Ideologies of Theory: Essays 1971–1986*, 2 vols (London: Routledge).

Kenny, Paul (1992) *Carry on Arguing: Literary-Historical Exchange and the Politics of Persuasion*, unpublished typescript, King's College, London.

Korzybski, Alfred (1948) *Science and Sanity: an Introduction to Non-Aristotelian Systems* (Lakeville, Ct.: International Non-Aristotelian Library Publishing Co.).

Lentricchia, Frank (1980) *After the New Criticism* (Chicago: University of Chicago Press).

— — (1982) 'Reading history with Kenneth Burke', in White and Brose (1982), 119–49.

— — (1983) *Criticism and Social Change* (Chicago and London: University of Chicago Press).

— — (1989) 'Analysis of Burke's speech by Frank Lentricchia', in Melia and Simons (1989), 281–96.

Melia, Trevor and Simons, Herbert (eds) (1989) *The Legacy of Kenneth Burke* (Madison: University of Wisconsin Press).

Nelson, Cary (1989) 'Writing as the accomplice of language: Kenneth Burke and poststructuralism', in Melia and Simons (1989), 156–73.

Rueckert, William H. (ed.) (1969) *Critical Responses to Kenneth Burke 1924–1966* (Minneapolis: University of Minnesota Press).

— — (1982) *Kenneth Burke and the Drama of Human Relations*, 2nd edn (Berkeley, Los Angeles and London: University of California Press).

Saluszinsky, Imre (1987) *Criticism in Society* (London and New York: Methuen), 209–40.

Schlauch, Margaret (1969) 'Review of *Attitudes Toward History*', in Rueckert (1969), 106–9.

Shelley, Percy Bysshe (1988) *Shelley's Prose; or, The Trumpet of a Prophecy*, ed. David Lee Clark (London: Fourth Estate). First published in 1954.

Southwell, Samuel B. (1987) *Kenneth Burke and Martin Heidegger, With a Note Against Deconstructionism*, University of Florida Humanities Monographs 60 (Gainesville, Fla.: University of Florida Press).

White, Hayden and Brose, Margaret (eds) (1982) *Representing Kenneth Burke: Selected Papers from the English Institute*, n.s., no. 6 (Baltimore and London: Johns Hopkins University Press).

Index

Entries in italics are titles of works by Burke except where otherwise noted. Entries for books by Burke are sub-divided by title of section or chapter.

121